NIGERIAN PROMISING ERA

UNLOCKING THE HIDDEN TREASURES

CHRISTOPHER OKOLI

Published by:

Good Faith Publishing Company

3420 Quannah Drive

Grand Prairie, Texas 75052

Email Address: cokoli2000@gmail.com

Telephone: 972 697 6013

Cover Design and Book Layout by **D3 Graphic Design**

This book is dedicated to President Barack Obama and the European Union in addition to the Nigerians who lost their precious lives while attempting to exercise their rights during the March 28th and April 12th Nigerian General Elections. One day, Nigerians will recognize the ultimate sacrifices you made for the nation. You are truly modern Nigerian heroes and eventually will be recognized accordingly.

To all the brave men and women of God, especially Rev. Father Frank Ejike Mbaka who was the first to openly preached against the evils of the outgoing government that made many Nigerians to support the opposition party

CONTENTS

CHAPTER 1

Introduction

The story of Nigeria ever since the colonial master left the country has been a more vicious cycle than progressive growth, because that basket of economic indexes of the country for the past 30 years is one of the worst economic indexes in the global village. Nigerians are very ignorant of their endless predicament; chronic corruption, the deadliest form of corruption, was systematically and structurally configured in the constitution to make sure that the country would never rise to lead Africa to greatness. African colonial masters used chronic corruption to divide and conquer the continent which made colonization easy.

Many centuries ago, the aggressively-expanding European empires identified Nigeria and other African countries as major profitable sources in building their nations; Africa then became the perfect and ideal solution as a cheap work force. Europeans were unsuited to the climate of Africa and suffered many tropical diseases. Occupying Nigeria and other African countries was not much of an option, so the Europeans found solace in exporting Africans to the global village. Decades of non-productiveness have made millions of Nigerians have to pay their ways out of the continent in search of jobs and better quality of lives.

Nigeria is undoubtedly one of the most populous countries in the world with over 170 million people and has a great potential to be the next engine of global village. The country is still experiencing the traumas of the national building process as chronic corruption continues to destroy all the democratic institutions and dividends from previous political dispensations. There is corruption in every country of the world. That said most countries only have 5% -10% of citizens engaged in large-scale fraudulent activities, making it a manageable level allowing growth to continue in such countries. Nigeria, however, suffers from chronic corruption.

Chronic corruption will be discussed in detail to show how it had retarded and destroyed all the promising leaders the country has ever found. In an interview with *CNN News* reporter Christian Amampor during his campaign, the new President Muhammadu Buhari said, "Nigeria must kill corruption or corruption will kill Nigeria." The current president is the only known Nigerian capable of winning the war on corruption. Nigerians should be grateful to the foreign policies of president Barrack Obama and some European Nations that helped Nigerian voices to be heard in the March 28th presidential election.

A failed effort from Nigerian military boys in 1966 to decisively kill corruption rapidly growing among the political class resulted in a prolonged civil war from 1967 to 1970. At the end of the civil war, the once cherished centralized and indivisible nation had become a divisively balkanized and disunited country. 45 years after the civil war, the country still has not been able to reconcile, resolve, and restore the spirit of love and harmony that existed prior to the civil war. As a result of the orchestrated divisions in the country, tribal sentiments replaced both national ethos and some individuals and tribes who were indirectly encouraged to emigrate out of the country. All Nigerians must join the new president who has indicated a genuine intention to conquer chronic corruption. He cannot win the battle without unflagging encouragement and total support from the masses.

There was mass exodus from Nigeria to all parts of the global village in the early 80s shortly after the boom and burst in the price of crude oil in the international market; the mass exodus was more visible in Nigerian minority groups who were still licking their sour wounds from corrupt politicians induced civil war. The fact that the mass exodus was not actually planned by the government to expose her greater tomorrows to western technologies, has now made it a nightmare to lure back those Nigerian professionals in Diaspora that left the country as youths. The truth still remains that Nigeria cannot become a true and indomitable giant of Africa; if majority of Nigerian professionals in Diaspora cannot be encouraged to be partakers in the national rebirth.

What is the place of Nigeria in the contest of the great contemporary historical continuum, the imperatives of which are defined in terms of large-scale socio-economic and political mutations? Based on the dialectics of history and the forces that are currently shaping a rapidly technological transformation of the universe, it would not be an overstatement to say that Nigeria has minimal future possibilities, considering the way the country is currently exhausting its resources due to chronic corruption. Chronic corruption is a very powerful battle that all Nigerians must join their forces together and win the battle, it must be conquered or the country might be history.

In terms of modern Nigerian history, one must ask whether the different degrees of socio-political traumas are inevitable consequences or the end product of a shaping process, or the repetitive patterns of past tragedies. These traumas could also be signs that Nigeria cannot be a viably productive country for herself and her diverse people, not to mention a great country respected by the rest of the world, until the war against chronic corruption is won.

It might be true that Nigeria was not created by the free effort and will of autonomously existing nationalities through deliberately articulate needs. The sub-assumption of the sovereignty of the various peoples of what is today called Nigeria is, to say the least, a historical accident motivated by the colonial masters' divisive strategies because of their selfish interests. Most of Nigeria's proclaimed independence exists only on paper because in reality the country still depends on Great Britain, her respected and powerful colonial master, for her livelihood. Of course Great Britain invested heavily in making sure that Nigerians were civilized and shown the path to greatness, so if the leaders decide to envelop the entire nation in chronic corruption, then the colonial master must be exonerated from all blames.

Nigeria might have been created as a convenient tool of colonial imperialism for the centralization of administrative machinery and officious policy of economic exploitation and political manipulations. Thus the foundation of Nigeria was buried not in affirmation of loyalty and goodwill of national desire, but in the objectification of the goals, philosophies and ideologies of external forces. However, the only visible feature in a modern Nigeria is a value system that glorifies a political class that loots the nation's wealth, a system that empowers the mediocre at the detriment of functionally and professionally managed institutions, and a system that elevates those who loot the nation's treasuries, while relegating the professionals. In a nutshell, the current status of the country is a broken system that is much closer to a failed state. Can the new president save the country? Absolutely he has done it before and there is no doubt that with the support of many Nigerians that are tired of chronic corruption, he will surely do it again.

"Things fall apart; the center cannot hold; mere anarchy is loose upon the world". This is a quote from Chinue Achebe, one of the greatest African writers, in a book titled *Things Fall Apart*. Although the book has outlived the author, it is a summary of what is going on in Nigeria today. After about seven decades of the book, modern Nigeria still faces the same terribly powerful monster that is threatening the co-existence of the giant of Africa. Nigerians have been religiously divided down to the basic human foundation that held the country together. Love, peace, and harmony no longer exist among the contemporary states, local government areas, towns, villages, clans, and churches; the divisions are in fact most pronounced in modern-day Nigerian families.

American President John F. Kennedy, one of the most inspirational and influential people in the history of the world once told Americans, "Ask not what your country can do for you, but what you can do for your country". Yes! Even though he was talking about the United States, the same could be true in Nigeria. "What you can do to help make Nigeria a better place? One of my university professors once told me, "You can get everything you want in life; if you will only help other people get what they want".

It would be great to see this book become a vessel that would help to resuscitate and revitalize those good spirits of love that were once inherent among Nigerians before the colonial era. All Nigerians must have to make painful sacrifices if they truly desire a great nation. Contrary to what the majority of Nigerians are thinking, Nigerian leaders actually are not the problems of the great nation; rather the masses who are chronically corrupt are the ones producing bad leaders. Therefore, meaningful and everlasting change will come to Nigeria when the masses purge themselves of chronic corruption in order to produce good leaders.

Understanding Chronic Corruption

Chronic corruption in this context means that corruption has degenerated to a level where the majority of Nigerians have seen corruption as an acceptable way of getting by in the country. It is like corruption has been indirectly legalized since it is difficult to find a true Nigerian without a corrupt mind. The new government will definitely run into some difficulties trying to put a cabinet together. Although the new president and his vice-president are men of integrity and unquestionable characters, what about their subordinates that would be working together for the benefit of the country. Would they be able to find some good men? The new leadership team must make sure that the losing political parties are motivated and encouraged to form a strong and formidable opposition party to help the government fight chronic corruption in the country.

Let us start by taking a good look at how chronic corruption has devastated the country through endless increases in the petrol price, because the stage is now set for another possible fuel increase. , a possible ticking time bomb for the incoming government

History of fuel price increases in Nigeria from 1973 to 2015:

Gowon, 1973: 6k to 8.45k (40.8%)

Murtala, 1976: 8.45k to 9k (0.59%)

Obasanjo, October 1, 1978: 9k to 15.3k (70%)

Shagari, April 20, 1982: 15.3k to 20k (30.71%)

Buhari December 1983 – August 1985 20k unchanged (0%)

Babangida, March 31 1986: 20k to 39.5k (97.5%)

Babangida, April 10 1988: 39.5k to 42k (6.33%)

Babangida, January 1, 1989: 42k to 60k Private vehicles.

Babangida, December 19, 1989: moved to uniform price of 60k (42.86%)

Babangida, March 6, 1991: 60k to 70k (16.67%)

Shonekan, November 8, 1993: 70k to ₦5 (614%)

Abacha, November 22, 1993: petrol price drops from ₦5 to ₦3.25k (-35%)

Abacha, October 2, 1994: ₦3.25k to ₦15 (361.54%)

Abubakar, December, 20, 1998: ₦11 to ₦25 (127.27%)

Abubakar, January 6, 1999: ₦25 to ₦20 (-20%)

Obasanjo, June 1, 2000: May 27th 2007 ₦20 to ₦75 (275%)

Yar'Adua, June 2007 from: ₦ 75 to N65 (-15.38%)

Jonathan, January 1, 2012: between ₦65 to ₦97 (49%)

A summary of the historical petrol price increases shows a compounded increase that is too scary for any human being to comprehend because is so outrageous and should not continue. Chronic corruption increased petrol price from mere **6 kobo in 1973 to ₦97 in 2015** in a span of 42 years petrol price has increased over **16, 160,000%.** This is happening in a country that has an abundance of crude oil. The currency Naira has also been devalued from the exchange rate of **₦0.66 to $1** in **1973 to ₦199 to $1 (30,051%) in 42 years**. Nigerians can no longer afford to not kill chronic corruption this time around, because in the next 40 years, the exchange rate might be ₦5,000 to $1, going by the historical trend of corrupt practices.

In the early 1980s in Nigeria, corruption only infested about 25% of the populace because the masses were very scared to give or receive bribes. Today in the country, civil servants are very bold to accept or give bribes in order to get whatever they want. Who said that a nation can be built in such environments where corruption has been legalized? Nigerians must accept the fact that Nigeria is very dear to the new president, and that was why he waited this long to have the opportunity to showcase his ability to fight and win the war on chronic corruption. Chronic corruption has given birth to the following: human trafficking, higher unemployment rate, higher crime rate, many militant groups, religious fanaticisms, hate groups, unstable polity, systematic failures, insecurity, kidnappings, armed robberies, unabated embezzlements, political monster individuals, organized crime families, etc.

The magnitude of chronic corruption in Nigeria today really needs honest, willing, committed, tenacious, unselfish, untiring, unrelenting and dedicated team players to confront and win the battle. The president's choice of deputy, a devoted, loving, caring and powerful man of God actually confirms his readiness to combat this deadly monster. Make no mistake, chronic corruption is very deadly and powerful, because past leaders that have tried to combat the cancer were rudely humiliated. The President is very ready for this powerful monster, because he is the only general that is going to the battlefield with an anointed man of God, and anyone who thinks that this regiment will be rudely humiliated needs to hold their breath, because the team has what it takes to win this battle. Nonetheless, Nigerians should not crucify their past leaders because they were conquered by the powerful battle of chronic corruption; if only the masses were bold enough to ask questions and support their genuine initiatives in moving the country forward, chronic corruption would be a thing of the past. Make sure that you give your unflagging support to this new team of political soldiers, because the unintended consequences of the team's failure will definitely place the country on uncharted territories.

Previous Nigerian leaders were merely agents used by chronic corruption owners to devastate the country's economy; therefore, the masses should stop pointing their fingers at them in other to eradicate chronic corruption in the country. The past leaders should be forgiven, and the new government should not dwell so much on trying to probe the past leaders to the fullest, because their unseen hands might plunge the country into uncharted territory. Here are some of the devastating economic and financial imbalances created by chronic corruption in Nigeria: human trafficking, higher unemployment rate, religious fanaticism, unstable polity, tribal interests and colossal systematic failure.

Human trafficking is defined as an act of recruiting, transferring or receiving a person through use of force, coercion or other means for the purpose of exploiting that individual. Trafficking is a lesser degree of the age long slavery, but chronic corruption has brought it back with so much force. When the leaders that were entrusted with the nation's wealth mismanaged and embezzled resources meant for the entire nation, the poor masses had no option other than to offer themselves for possible human trafficking. The victims (young girls) more often are people experiencing chronic corruption—wrecked families that are trying to get back on their feet again. Human traffickers can be individual pimps, gangs, criminal networks, small business owners, factory owners, corporations, brothels, massage parlor managers, or employers of domestic servants. Both men and women are involved in trafficking operations, and they all profit from the control, exploitation and misery of others. Despite some progress, the number of traffickers caught and convicted remains low, because of poor anti-trafficking legislation, corruption, and lack of training among law enforcement officials and prosecutors. Victims may also be unwilling to cooperate because their traffickers have threatened to kill their loved ones. There is human trafficking all over the world because human beings are always ready to exploit the needy humans, but the magnitude of traffickers in Nigeria and other African countries is overwhelming because of chronic corruption.

Higher unemployment rate: the same chronic corruption that motivates and encourages Nigerian leaders to run the country as their own has created huge labor imbalance in the country, because the unemployment rate among Nigerian youths is around 60%. Close to one million Nigerians graduate every year from the nation's higher learning institutions, and after their national youth service corps (a mandatory one year service in the country) the majority of them go back to their respective families because there are not enough jobs for them. Meanwhile, the looted treasury from Nigeria is taken outside the country for hidden investments for the leaders' retirement needs. How long can the country continue to brew youths without future and opportunities to give them a chance to contribute in building the nation? Muhammadu Buhari is a leader that is capable of ending the massive looting that has been wrecking the collective future of the masses. Nigerians and other Africans have turned the Mediterranean Sea, the entry point into Europe a mass graveyard because the boats they followed to run away into a new world where they can at least have the basic inevitability of live also get capsized on that particular spot.

Religious fanaticism: When the youths are deprived of the opportunity to be part of the nation builders, the country makes them vulnerable to be exploited by the men of the underground economy, tribal militants, political thugs and religious insurgent groups. All these deadly vices will definitely continue to grow in Nigeria and other African countries until African leaders embrace good governance. If Europeans and other civilized countries are really worried about the increasing deaths of innocent Africans running away from chronic corrupt infested countries, they should help to kill chronic corruption in those countries and save those lives.

Actually, what the world is witnessing in Lampedusa (death trap for African immigrants) today is the unintended consequences of an age-long colonization tool that was used to divide and conquer Africans which was never restored before the colonial masters left the shores of Africa. If things are okay in Africa, why would Africans risk their lives trying to get away from the shores of Africa to unknown places. Enough is enough! Either Europeans help the poor masses of Africa reclaim their countries or start producing good, corrupt-free leaders or European countries' safety will not be guaranteed because of those immigrants that they are allowing into their countries.

Unstable polity: The colonial masters' philosophy is that if you cannot divide any group of people, you can never conquer them nor control them. Chronic corruption is an instrument of division that Nigeria and other African countries are using to prevent the poor masses from joining forces against the leaders. The unintended consequences of massive deployment of chronic corruption for division have made it impossible for Nigerians to see themselves as Nigerians because their leaders in the quest of manipulating them have made the poor masses to rather identify with their ethnic groups. That is why a population of over 170 million people cannot really boast of up to 10,000 Nigerians. When Nigerian leaders are not dividing the poor masses with religious sentiments, they use tribal and ethnic sentiments, making it impossible for the country to develop "common interest" that is a key ingredient in nation building.

Tribal interests: chronic corruption makes it difficult for over 170 million people in Nigeria to think of Nigeria first, because all their allegiance goes to tribal and ethnic groups; as a result of the divisions the political leaders instituted looting in the country for their own interest. If the president of the country is chronically corrupt, that is not their business because the president is from their tribe and they are ready to defend him with their last breath. No one can build a nation with such level of division that is prevalent in Nigeria today, because nation building requires more than tribal ethos and ethnic orientations.

Colossal systematic failure: chronic corruption has destroyed all the democratic institutions left behind by the colonial master of Nigeria, and without restoring those institutions, it will be very difficult for good governance to thrive in the country. Nigeria was in fact much closer to a failed state because militant groups, armed robbers, kidnappers and other religious fanatics were getting more powerful than the security apparatus the government has in place. How can over 200 Nigerian school girls kidnapped in broad daylight from a boarding school, still today have not been found?

America sent few military personnel into Nigeria to help in finding those girls, but when it dawned on the Americans that the level of chronic corruption in the country would not help to find and bring the girls back to their parents, they simply had to leave the country. Oh! President Muhammadu Buhari, honestly Nigerians must constantly pray and support you because chronic corruption has eaten so deep into the blood of the average Nigerian that it might be very difficult for you to constitute your cabinet. Nonetheless, if anybody in the country can battle chronic corruption and come out alive, you are definitely the right person because you have done it in the past and with the help of God, you shall conquer and overcome this great evil that has been ravaging Nigeria for decades.

CHAPTER 2

Enabling Laws for Wealth Creation

Unlocking the social assets in villages

Nigerians have billions of dollars buried in their villages in the form of developed homes that have only social and traditional values, because they can neither borrow nor sell those village homes since the homes have no economic values. The villages are the only places in Nigeria where undeveloped properties are worth more that developed properties because the developed homes have no resale value. The villages/towns are also not directly included in the power and revenue-sharing formula in the country, as the towns/villages rely on whatever the governors or local government chairmen decides to give them. This is actually the primary reason all the towns and villages are not financially and economically viable entities. If Nigerian lawmakers can constitutionally empower the towns/villages to democratically elect custodians for the towns/villages, then the elected officials will now have borrowing and taxing powers to start developing the towns/villages. The growth and economic viability of Nigeria will depend on how the new government would encourage constitutional amendments that would empower the towns/villages to unlock the hidden assets in the towns/villages by allowing these remote places to be run by elected mayors and councilors that would have binding powers to go out and negotiate businesses, borrow funds and tax the residents.

Webster defined democracy as "government of the people by the people for the people." Based on this philosophy the Nigerian forefathers elected to adopt this system of government but the political class (politicians) has actually omitted the key principle of democracy which is the "people." As a result the democratic institutions in the country are yearning for transparent political reforms to sustain democracy in the country. Nigerian democracy never made it all the way to the grassroots, where the representation of the people started, because the military regime that forced the hurried-up ideology to the political class did not allow the politicians enough time to figure out if they were conservatives or liberals. Nonetheless, the existence of over 28 political parties in Nigeria definitely would not help the growth of political ideologies and democratic institutions in the country, because in order for democracy to thrive in any nation a strong opposition party would need to act as a watch dog to the ruling party. Nigeria definitely needs only two political parties if the country really wishes to sustain democracy in the country, because all these parties are adding credence to a divided group of people that cannot and do not want to work together. Having only two political parties in Nigeria would definitely help to encourage the unifying process of the diverse tribal and ethnic groups in the country.

Nigerians would definitely be happy to see the People's Democratic Party (PDP) play the opposition role to help the new ruling party All Peoples Congress (APC) fight corruption in the country. As the new president Muhammadu Buhari's nomenclature is definitely Corruption Killer, he still needs a strong opposition party to help him fight and win the battle of chronic corruption. He is definitely the only known Nigerian that has the tenacity to conquer the chronic corruption that is devastating everything that Nigerians are once known for. Chronic corruption is deadly and any nation that fails to kill it will definitely be killed by chronic corruption.

To all Nigerians, the danger is clear and immediate; therefore all Nigerians must start making sacrifices to wrestle their beloved country back from chronic corruption before the situation gets terribly worst. This is definitely not the time to apportion blames because over 95% of Nigerians contributed immensely to the fast growth of chronic corruption in the country. Some Nigerians failed to speak out, while others were financially, tribally or sentimentally induced to aid and abate in the perpetuation and escalation of chronic corruption in the country. Nigeria undoubtedly was at the verge of being killed by chronic corruption, and unless Nigerians join the new president (a known and tested individual with anti-corruption stand) in an aggressive war against chronic corruption, then the country might not be together long enough to tell the story. It is not about the past leaders that have gone through the leadership mantles of the country; it is about one of the inherited tools that were used by the colonial masters to capture their territories during the colonial dark ages. A tool that were used to financially induce ethnic tribes against others, wives against husbands and politicians against their followers. Nigeria must let go of this deadly tool because the application of the tool will always lead to chronic corruption that eventually end in balkanization of such countries.

The colonial masters actually did wonderful and commendable works in Africa- Nigeria inclusive, they brought civilization to the people and stopped some of the deadly cultures that Nigerians were practicing then, (killing of twins and burying a king with 7 human beings), but Nigerians must reject using the deadly tool of corruption because once it turns into chronic corruption, it becomes difficult to combat. The politicians shared millions of bags of rice and other items to Nigerians to get the masses to vote one way or the other during the just concluded presidential election that took place in the country. Why? These campaigning actions that could be defined as legalized bribery have been repeatedly carried out in the country for decades. The masses always send the politicians to banks to borrow billions of Naira (Nigerian currency), and when the politicians engage in such acts, they know that if they fail to win the election, their lives would not have much value left in a failure outcome of such elections. The elections now become lives or deaths situation for Nigerian politicians, because of accepted corrupt practices. The Nigerian masses really need to stop destroying their promising leaders by not taking bribes or compensatory promises from the politicians in other to get the best out of the politicians. If there are no takers, definitely the givers will stop, for corruption to take place; there must be a giver and a take. So why are all the fingers pointing to the political class, while the masses continue to encourage the politicians to loot the treasury and commit chronic corruption at the same time? If Nigerians fail to give their newly elected officials the maximum support they need to start the process that would eliminate chronic corruption in the country, then what happened to the past elected officials would happen to the new group. Nigerians must say NO to chronic corruption to remain relevant in the new world order.

All Nigerians must be willing to go through some painful and transparent reforms that must come as result of genuine efforts that would help to eradicate chronic corruption in the country. Make no mistake about the present condition of the country because the current beneficiaries of the chronic corruption would unleash baseless and unjustified attacks on the integrity of any person trying to declare war on chronic corruption. Please be ready to support the leaders that would attack chronic corruption from all positions, because they really need your support to secure the future of the country from those political vultures circling around the new leaders now.

Nigerians might have voted for President Muhammadu Buhari because of his previous attempt to eradicate corruption in the 1980s. Some of the older people remembered when chronic corruption was surging unabated in the 1980s and Buhari showed up and declared War against Indiscipline (WAI). The program was so successful that Nigerians started behaving like decent people once again. Expectations were very high that the new president knew how to fight and win war against corruption (corruption begets indiscipline), so an average man can be very sure that Nigerians are waiting for more "War against Corruption (WAC)". The newly- elected political class needs your compliance and above all your prayers to help fight and eradicate chronic corruption in the country. Nigerians should remember that even the past religious leaders who tried to speak out against corruption were all labeled anti-Nigerian, and some of them even received death threats. Let the masses purge themselves first of chronic corruption and then join the new political leaders in restoring sanity in all the democratic institutions that have been devastated in the country.

Nigerian government currently runs one of the most expensive tri-levels of government in federal, state, and local areas (county equivalent). The towns/villages where the masses reside were invariably omitted from the government equation of power sharing. The world can now understand why towns/villages are not economically and financially viable in Nigeria because the constitution never recognizes their important roles in nation building.

A democratic system of government recommends three branches of merely equal powers for check and balances on the executive, legislative and judiciary to help balance power and prevent abuses in the system. If any of these branches is weak, democracy finds it very difficult to function because one of the core values of democracy has been broken. In the Nigerian democratic setting, the executive is the only branch of the government that is horribly, abusively and chronically powerful at the expense of the judiciary and legislative arm of the government. In fact, it is more of a civilian dictatorial type of government. Nigerian constitution only empowers the following:

A. Federal government, whose President and the sole custodian of all the federating states guarantees that security, financial, economic and social needs of the states are adequately addressed by this unit of government. For the interest of all the states, the president of Nigeria was constitutionally empowered to enter into any loan agreement, treaty, or contracts that would be binding to all the states. Legislators are also drawn from all the states to help make laws and review the constitution of the land to make sure that they are in tandem with the citizens' constantly changing needs. The Judiciary was also there to make sure the laws and constitutions are well interpreted the ways the law makers and the founding fathers designed them to work. The federal government is using military forces to secure and protect the country against any external aggression while using the police force to maintain internal peace and tranquility.

B. State governments' custodians are called governors, whose sole responsibility is making sure that security, financial, economic and social needs of the local government areas in their respective states are adequately addressed by this unit of government. The state laws also empower the governors to enter into any external or internal loan agreements, or contracts for the sole interest of all the local government areas being represented by the states. Legislators are also drawn from all the local government areas of the state to help make laws and review the laws of the state to make sure that they are in tandem with the citizens' constantly changing needs.

The Judiciary was also established to make sure the laws and constitutions are well interpreted, the ways the law makers and the state founding fathers designed them to work. The states are completely deprived the opportunity of establishing their own security apparatus as the Nigerian police force was saddled with this task. Empowering state governors to secure their own states would have made Nigerian governors accountable for insecurity in their states. State governors should be made accountable for security lapses in their respective states, since the constitution of the land apportioned huge amount of money monthly to the governors for unquestionable and unaccountable security needs.

C. Local area governments' custodians are called "local government area chairmen "with the sole responsibility of making sure that the security, financial, economic and social needs of the towns/villages in their respective local government areas are adequately addressed by this unit of government. The Constitution should have also empowered the local government area chairmen to enter into any external or internal loan agreements, or contracts for the sole interest of all the towns/villages being represented on the local government areas. Councilors are also drawn from some of the towns/villages to help make laws and review the ordinances of the local government areas to make sure that they are in tandem with the citizens' constantly changing needs.

The Judiciary should also be established to make sure the ordinances are well interpreted. The local government area chairmen were also deprived of opportunity that would have made them accountable for insecurity in their local government areas. Is it not about time that Nigerians get to know why state governors and local government area chairmen are completely exonerated from security lapses in their respective managing areas?

Electing Town/Village Officials

The greatest omission in the tenet of Nigerian democracy was the non-inclusion of the towns/villages from the constitution of the land and the non-exercising rights of the towns/villages under the country's power and revenue sharing formulas. How can the federal, state, local government areas, constitutionally empowered by CEOs (President, Governors and Chairmen) to economically, financially and socially manage those levels of governments, and not assign any CEOs to the foundation of democracy (Towns/Villages)? This is a costly omission that must be addressed immediately if Nigeria as a nation can play the giant role that Africa is asking it. Accountability must start from the grassroots by an urgent constitutional empowerment of the towns/villages to democratically elect their CEOs in the same manner as the other levels of governments elect their own CEOs. Addressing the shortfall of the towns/Villages would immediately create over eight million jobs in Nigeria. Assumptions are as follows:

800 local government areas in the country

100 average Towns/Villages in each Local Government Area

One hundred workers in each Town/Village (Chairman, councilors, Judiciary workers, etc.

Do the simple math: **800 * 100 = 80,000 * 100 = 8,000,000** gainful employments. This number would definitely help to solve the huge unemployment lapses in the country, and would be a big positive bang on the GDP of the country. Can one imagine eight million people receiving monthly income, which would later be reinvested into the economy?

This is where the towns/villages addition in the power-sharing formula in the country gets very interesting because the benefits completely outweigh any disadvantages. The towns/villages would now have their own budgets, thereby monetizing most of the non-performing assets in towns in order to generate revenues. Towns and villages will now make enough revenues through taxes and fines rather than depending solemnly on crude oil revenue that is actually declining. For many centuries, the towns/villages have been left at the mercies of the Emirs, Obas, Igwes and other traditional rulers without constitutional empowerment of financial and economic welfare of the dwellers. Nigerian legislators should quickly pass the law that would empower the towns/villages to be managed by a democratically elected mayors and cabinet members that would see to the financial, economic and social needs of towns/villages, while the Emirs, Kabiasi, and Igwes and other traditional heads are made cultural custodians and ceremonial leaders.

The Constitution should not necessarily do away with the traditional rulers (custodians), just allow them to maintain and run the traditional affairs of the towns while the democratically elected leaders of the towns have constitutional powers to go and negotiate financing and funding on behalf of the towns and at the same time, compete with other towns to bring businesses in their areas.

This is one of the biggest conundrums of Nigerian government for not being able to create enough employment for the growing youth. The omission of towns/villages from Nigerian constitutions is depriving the creation of millions of jobs the country really needs to get to the path of greatness. The omission might have been one of the unintended consequences of the past dictators in effort to manipulate wealth of the entire nations.

Land Use Acts

The executive branch, legislature, and judiciary should make sure that whatever changes were made to the land use act in the 1970s must be revised with immediate effect, because this action would put the country on path to greatness. The emergence of towns/villages as power sharing institutions would help to make the Nigerian towns and villages economically and financially viable in the country. Many communities in Nigeria today simply contribute monies to build churches, schools, pipe-borne water systems, and roads when they have state and local governments that are supposed to be doing these projects for them. It is time that Nigerians engage in intellectual debates that would tower the giant above many nations in this world. Towns/Villages need high levels of financial engineering to start making them productive and viable entities.

Giving the land back to the villages and towns would unlock the trillions of dollars hidden in those villages. They would be able to tax property owners in those areas to generate revenue that would be use in the day-to-day operations. The revenues would help to build and develop those areas as modern dwelling environments. Many Nigerians are maintaining two homes today which would not help to put the country on the path of greatness, because those beautiful mansions in the villages only have social value and not economic value; the landed properties built in villages only have social values that really helped in destroying Nigerian value systems.

The elected village officers would then evaluate the properties and undeveloped lands in their respective villages and assess taxes accordingly. The village officials can also pass ordinances that would stop some Nigerians from burying loved ones in their homes, because such acts destroy the economic value of any developed or undeveloped properties. All villages must have functional burying grounds where their loved ones could be sent for burials, and in so doing, the surviving relatives can also sell or borrow money with such properties. A built-up burial ground would probably create jobs for about eight of the villagers and be professionally managed to generate revenues to the village.

All parts of Nigeria must be motivationally encouraged to be financially independent and the reversing of whatever land use policy that took the land away from villages needs urgent attention. Nigeria's march to greatness must definitely start from the grassroots where millions of gainful employments can be created, and at the same time wrestle many youths away from under-ground economy and militant groups. How can a country like Nigeria be financially independent without adequate and knowledgeable personnel to create financial engineering in the country? Nigeria has many underperforming and nonperforming assets that must be unlocked and converted into performing assets that would create unimaginable wealth to help the country navigate through the inevitable, fast-approaching austerity measures.

CHAPTER 3

Unifying the Politically Divided Tribes

Ever since the colonial masters left the shores of Nigeria, the unity of the country has been on a downward trajectory, because the master left with the absolute secret of control. Less than seven years after her master's exit, Nigeria was embroiled in a deadly three-year civil war that took the lives of over a million Nigerians, and destroyed properties valued at over fifty million British pounds.

Where would the financial and economic dexterity of Nigeria be today without the damages of the civil war? The unity of Nigerian ethnic groups was broken, many lives were lost and a large number of assets vanished from the emerging giant of Africa; it is quite unfortunate that the healing of the deadly civil war has not been completed yet, because one of the major ethnic tribes involved in that civil war has been relegated from the second position to distant last in the country. People that fail to study their history tend to forget, and when they forget, chances are very high that they will repeat the same deadly mistakes that generated the history in the first place.

Nigeria's civil war was caused by the unseen hands of chronic corruption; young and naïve army officers (unfortunately from one tribe) tried to eradicate chronic corruption from the country, when the politicians connived with some other officers and turned the table on them. Story has it that the young officers were not happy the way the politicians were embezzling money, so they planned a coup to kill all the chronically corrupt politicians. However, one of the officers chronically infected thwarted the efforts of the others by failing to kill the politician who was from the same tribal group of the young officers. Therefore, the politicians were able to turn the tables around.

Develop Sports for Unity

A sport might be defined as an organized, competitive, entertaining and skillful activity requiring commitment, strategy, and fair play, in which a winner can be defined by objective means. It is based on mental readiness and physical athleticism of the competitors trying to overcome opponents. Nonetheless, sporting events like chess, checkers, board and card games are sometimes classified as "games of the mind" but frankly speaking "sport" by itself refers to some physical activity. Non-competitive activities may also qualify as sporting events; for example, jogging, hide and seek, tug of war, or playing catch are usually classified as forms of recreational activities; they may also be informally called "sports" because of their similarity to competitive games.

Sports are governed by a set of rules, standard or customs established by the founders of such sports. Physical events such as scoring goals, touchdowns, baskets, points or crossing a line first often define the result of a sport. However, the degree of skill and performance in some sports such as diving, dressage, and figure-skating are judged according to well-defined criteria. Nonetheless, sporting events like talent-search, body building and beauty pageant competitions are judged differently because skill does not have to be displayed by contestants.

Records are kept and updated for most sports at the highest levels, while failures and accomplishments are widely announced in sports news. Sports are most often played just for fun or for the simple fact that people need exercise to stay in good physical condition. However, professional sports are a major source of entertainment to the fans and a source of financial compensation to the participants and owners (organizers) of those sporting events. Sports can also be sources of employment to the populace, revenue (taxes) to government, investment to owners, etc.

While sporting events may vary, participants are expected to display wonderfully acquired skills, sportsmanship, and observe standards of conduct such as respect. Professional sports are an industry worth over two trillion American dollars globally. Nigeria and other African countries are not getting up to three percent (3%) of this huge global gold mine. This is not right, because if they can develop their professional sports to global standards, they can benefit from unifications, talent export, source of revenues, reduction in underground economic activities, reduction in cult activism in schools and job creations.

Unification

Ever since Nigeria and other Africa countries were divided by colonial masters for easy conquest, there has not been any known serious effort by either the colonial masters or Africans themselves to unite all the divided groups without putting their own conflicting interests first. The little unifying institutions that were left behind were religiously destroyed by African dictators in their own efforts to subdue and control the poor masses forever. Nigerians and the majority of Africans were bad followers because they watched as the dictators destroyed one ethnic group after the other.. Most Africans stopped speaking out about the face of evil. Nigeria and other African countries need help to rebuild and restore democratic institutions that would provide them with a noble and respected status. Sports should be seen as one of the best tools to accomplish the task of uniting Nigerians and other Africans because some made super-stars and stars would be used to promote peace and unity.

Chronic corruption has turned South Africans against their fellow Africans because they started killing non- South Africans from the town of Xenophobia in April 2015, whom they accused of taking away their jobs. People are now blaming the South Africans that are perpetuating the horrifying evils on their fellow Africans without looking beyond the killings. What if African leaders had not looted and embezzled the funds that were required to develop and create jobs in their respective countries, would there be so many job hunters from all over African fighting for few available jobs in South Africa? What if the South African government has been quickly engrossed in chronic corruption that the leaders followed the same mismanagement process? A further probe in South African government might have a chilling revelation to the world, so we should wait for the outcome of whatever investigation that is going on in that lovely country now.

It is about time the super-powers and the global village stop having selective amnesia to injustices being perpetuated in Nigeria and other under-developing countries. Our world is now a global village and every effort needs to be made in helping the countries that are behind. Nonetheless, Nigeria and other African countries cannot continue to wait on the global village before they can figure out the best ways to start uniting the divided tribes and ethnic groups. If Nigeria fails to institute programs or use of sports to promote unity in the country, then every effort any administration might make would be futile, because the level of divisions perpetuated by her colonial master and Nigerian dictators cannot allow the manifestation of "common interest" needed for nation building to take place.

Nigeria has a population of over 170 million people but would not boast of up to 10,000 Nigerians, because everyone in the country identifies with some tribes and not with overall Nigeria. Over 80% of the time, a Nigerian name identifies the tribal and ethnic orientation of that individual, thereby limiting the scope of potential association of the individual. On August 28, 1963, Martin Luther King, Jr. delivered his famous "I have a dream" speech. See the speech below and help stop the outrageous tribal, ethnic and religious divides in Nigeria.

"I am happy to join with you today in what will go down in history as the greatest demonstration for freedom in the history of our nation.

Five score years ago, a great American, in whose symbolic shadow we stand today, signed the Emancipation Proclamation. This momentous decree came as a great beacon light of hope to millions of Negro slaves who had been seared in the flames of withering injustice. It came as a joyous daybreak to end the long night of their captivity.

But one hundred years later, the Negro still is not free. One hundred years later, the life of the Negro is still sadly crippled by the manacles of segregation and the chains of discrimination. One hundred years later, the Negro lives on a lonely island of poverty in the midst of a vast ocean of material prosperity. One hundred years later, the Negro is still languished in the corners of American society and finds himself an exile in his own land. And so we've come here today to dramatize a shameful condition.

In a sense we've come to our nation's capital to cash a check. When the architects of our republic wrote the magnificent words of the Constitution and the Declaration of Independence, they were signing a promissory note to which every American was to fall heir. This note was a promise that all men, yes, black men as well as white men, would be guaranteed the "unalienable Rights" of "Life, Liberty and the pursuit of Happiness." It is obvious today that America has defaulted on this promissory note, insofar as her citizens of color are concerned. Instead of honoring this sacred obligation, America has given the Negro people a bad check, a check which has come back marked "insufficient funds."

But we refuse to believe that the bank of justice is bankrupt. We refuse to believe that there are insufficient funds in the great vaults of opportunity of this nation. And so, we've come to cash this check, a check that will give us upon demand the riches of freedom and the security of justice.

We have also come to this hallowed spot to remind America of the fierce urgency of Now. This is no time to engage in the luxury of cooling off or to take the tranquilizing drug of gradualism. Now is the time to make real the promises of democracy. Now is the time to rise from the dark and desolate valley of segregation to the sunlit path of racial justice. Now is the time to lift our nation from the quicksand of racial injustice to the solid rock of brotherhood. Now is the time to make justice a reality for all of God's children.

It would be fatal for the nation to overlook the urgency of the moment. This sweltering summer of the Negro's legitimate discontent will not pass until there is an invigorating autumn of freedom and equality. Nineteen sixty-three is not an end, but a beginning. And those who hope that the Negro needed to blow off steam and will now be content will have a rude awakening if the nation returns to business as usual. And there will be neither rest nor tranquility in America until the Negro is granted his citizenship rights. The whirlwinds of revolt will continue to shake the foundations of our nation until the bright day of justice emerges.

But there is something that I must say to my people, who stand on the warm threshold which leads into the palace of justice: In the process of gaining our rightful place, we must not be guilty of wrongful deeds. Let us not seek to satisfy our thirst for freedom by drinking from the cup of bitterness and hatred. We must forever conduct our struggle on the high plane of dignity and discipline. We must not allow our creative protest to degenerate into physical violence. Again and again, we must rise to the majestic heights of meeting physical force with soul force.

The marvelous new militancy which has engulfed the Negro community must not lead us to a distrust of all white people, for many of our white brothers, as evidenced by their presence here today, have come to realize that their destiny is tied up with our destiny. And they have come to realize that their freedom is inextricably bound to our freedom.

We cannot walk alone.

And as we walk, we must make the pledge that we shall always march ahead.

We cannot turn back.

There are those who are asking the devotees of civil rights, "When will you be satisfied?" We can never be satisfied as long as the Negro is the victim of the unspeakable horrors of police brutality. We can never be satisfied as long as our bodies, heavy with the fatigue of travel, cannot gain lodging in the motels of the highways and the hotels of the cities. We cannot be satisfied as long as the Negro's basic mobility is from a smaller ghetto to a larger one. We can never be satisfied as long as our children are stripped of their independence and robbed of their dignity by signs stating: "For Whites only." We cannot be satisfied as long as a Negro in Mississippi cannot vote and a Negro in New York believes he has nothing for which to vote. No, no, we are not satisfied, and we will not be satisfied until "justice rolls down like waters, and righteousness like a mighty stream."

I am not unmindful that some of you have come here out of great trials and tribulations. Some of you have come fresh from narrow jail cells. And some of you have come from areas where your quest - quest for freedom left you battered by the storms of persecution and staggered by the winds of police brutality. You have been the veterans of creative suffering. Continue to work with the faith that unearned suffering is redemptive. Go back to Mississippi, go back to Alabama, go back to South Carolina, go back to Georgia, go back to Louisiana, go back to the slums and ghettos of our northern cities, knowing that somehow this situation can and will be changed.

Let us not wallow in the valley of despair, I say to you today, my friends.

And so even though we face the difficulties of today and tomorrow, I still have a dream. It is a dream deeply rooted in the American dream.

26

I have a dream that one day this nation will rise up and live out the true meaning of its creed: "We hold these truths to be self-evident, that all men are created equal."

I have a dream that one day on the red hills of Georgia, the sons of former slaves and the sons of former slave owners will be able to sit down together at the table of brotherhood.

I have a dream that one day even the state of Mississippi, a state sweltering with the heat of injustice, sweltering with the heat of oppression, will be transformed into an oasis of freedom and justice.

I have a dream that my four little children will one day live in a nation where they will not be judged by the color of their skin but by the content of their character.

I have a dream today!

I have a dream that one day, down in Alabama, with its vicious racists, with its governor having his lips dripping with the words of "interposition" and "nullification" -- one day right there in Alabama little black boys and black girls will be able to join hands with little white boys and white girls as sisters and brothers.

I have a dream today!

I have a dream that one day every valley shall be exalted, and every hill and mountain shall be made low, the rough places will be made plain, and the crooked places will be made straight; "and the glory of the Lord shall be revealed and all flesh shall see it together."2

This is our hope, and this is the faith that I go back to the South with.

With this faith, we will be able to hew out of the mountain of despair a stone of hope. With this faith, we will be able to transform the jangling discords of our nation into a beautiful symphony of brotherhood. With this faith, we will be able to work together, to pray together, to struggle together, to go to jail together, to stand up for freedom together, knowing that we will be free one day.

And this will be the day -- this will be the day when all of God's children will be able to sing with new meaning:

My country 'tis of thee, sweet land of liberty, of thee I sing.

Land where my fathers died, land of the Pilgrim's pride,

From every mountainside, let freedom ring!

And if America is to be a great nation, this must become true.

And so let freedom ring from the prodigious hilltops of New Hampshire.

Let freedom ring from the mighty mountains of New York.

Let freedom ring from the heightening Alleghenies of Pennsylvania.

Let freedom ring from the snow-capped Rockies of Colorado.

Let freedom ring from the curvaceous slopes of California.

But not only that:

Let freedom ring from Stone Mountain of Georgia.

Let freedom ring from Lookout Mountain of Tennessee.

Let freedom ring from every hill and molehill of Mississippi.

From every mountainside, let freedom ring.

And when this happens, when we allow freedom ring, when we let it ring
from every village and every hamlet, from every state and every city, we
will be able to speed up that day when all of God's children, black men
and white men, Jews and Gentiles, Protestants and Catholics, will be able
to join hands and sing in the words of the old Negro spiritual:

Free at last! Free at last!

Thank God Almighty, we are free at last!"

What a speech! Nigeria can be great when Nigerians adhere to the
true meaning of this wonderful speech. The famous speech pierced
into the hearts of some American leaders that they decided to
confront the country's major challenge of racial divide immediately.
In the same vein, Nigerian leaders must confront the major challenge

of chronic corruption or ignore the fast global changing world at their own peril. Professional sports must be one of the next frontiers of growth in Nigeria because it breeds love and not racism or nepotism. Instead of Nigerian political leaders introducing unifying policies like sports, they are engrossed in using religion and other divisive strategies to destroy good loving Nigerians. Make no mistake—sports will be a bridge for unity only if the Nigerian government spends money and engages the services of qualified personnel to oversee sporting activities. Unity is panacea to Nigerian moving forward, but chronic corruption must be subdued and conquered at the same time, because the country cannot live up to her potential without confronting this important issue.

Sports breed unity, unity breeds team work, and team work breeds a unifying beautiful country with fewer militant groups. America and other developed countries have succeeded in turning sports like Basketball, Baseball, Boxing, Football, Ice-hockey and soccer into trillions of dollar businesses. Sports is over two trillion dollar venture providing employment for over three hundred million people globally. Nigeria needs to get out of the colonial and dictatorial enslavement syndromes and use sports to start bridging the decades of division..

The importance of professional sports to the social, racial, political and economic activities of America can never be adequately emphasized in this book. Without the advanced level of professional sports in America, nobody can say for sure if Martin Luther King Jr.'s dream would have come to reality today, because the super-stars that emerged from the sporting events were greatly respected and used for promoting unity in the country.

Racism would have still been in a higher level in America today, without the advanced development in professional sports. The racial divide in America and the global village would have made it impossible for our generation to witness Martin Luther King, Jr.'s "dream" come to fruition, when Barack Obama was sworn in on January 2009 as the 44th American president. True, racism and tribal sentiments exist in our world, but they are completely blinded by the fact that humans love winners while they emotionally sympathize with losers. The new administration in Nigeria definitely needs to create over ten million jobs within five years if democracy has to be sustained in the country. However, if the leaders embrace

29

the development of professional sports in the country, then five million jobs will automatically be created immediately. The Nigerian government definitely needs to look into the development of sports from primary to professional levels because in so doing, unifying ambassadors in form of superstars and stars would emerge.

Talent export

God gave each and every human being a unique gift that the public sometimes refers to as "talent." Individuals can learn any sport, but the super-stars are supernaturally gifted and spiritually packaged for that particular sport. Some examples are Michael Jordan of America who played basketball to perfection, or Pele of Brazil who helped define soccer. Millions of such people are in Nigeria and as such, Nigerian leaders have to put mechanisms in place to help discover such talents and even export some of them to the global village. Unfortunately, Nigerian leaders can never hatch such talented individuals because chronic corruption has already embezzled the funds that were set aside for their search. Also, tribal sentiments can never allow the officials to prudentially select a talented individual that is not from the same tribes with the officials.

Nigerian leaders just have to start thinking outside the box in order to save their leadership positions in the fast changing global village. For Nigerian leaders to achieve the type of talent search and discovery that is being discussed here, it will mean a near total overhauling of their educational systems, and the ministry of sports which the leaders might be reluctant to embrace. Change is always difficult to accept, especially when it entails giving up some political powers. Human beings sometimes are willing to resist change with the last drop of their blood. That is why there are more life-presidents in Africa than any other continent of our world. No nation can recreate the past greatness into the present without transparent changes, sacrifices and creative team work from all the stakeholders.

Catching talented individuals at young ages will definitely help the country in producing many local super-stars that can compete with other international super-stars. Nigerian leaders need to spend more resources on the future leaders of the country by grooming the kids at very tender ages. Development of all types of sports in Nigeria must start at the early ages, and the resources should come from cutting down the exorbitant salaries of political officers and their appointees. Personnel and equipment should be in place from the very first day a Nigerian or an African child steps into kindergarten, primary, secondary schools and continue into college. Political office holders and their appointees are taking home so much money in salaries and allowances, leaving nothing for capital expenditures in the country.

The new administration might consider cutting off about 50% of the huge political salaries as a starting point for fighting chronic corruption. Each Nigerian child should be adequately profiled and examined to find out where the talent is, and the child will be motivationally encouraged to fully develop that talent. In a country of over 170 million people, the chances are very high that at the end of every year, thousands of children can help further the unifying process of the country.

How many Nigerian tennis players are featured in any of the U.S. or European Opens every year? You cannot see one, because Nigerian leaders do not invest in building tennis courts or encourage young Nigerians to start playing and practicing at early ages. High schools do not have tennis courts, and the few universities that do have them in terrible shape. One can only harvest what he sows, and if the Nigerian government refuses to invest in sports, then the country will not benefit from trillions of dollars that other countries are enjoying today. Fans always overlook tribal sentiments, religious orientations and racial divides; as long as their superstar players are helping their teams win matches and perform to their expectations.. Sports will definitely help to revitalize the spirit of teamwork which will help to propel Nigeria into greatness and become the true giant of Africa, but Nigeria cannot develop sports without first eradicating chronic corruption.

Source of Revenues

Now that crude oil revenue will continue to stubbornly go down, there could not have been a better time for Nigerian government to cut the huge political salaries and invest the money in amateur and professional sports, to immensely benefit the country. The country could withstand the impending worse austerity measures with adequate diversification of the import-based economy of the country that is growing worse every day.

Nigeria must find ways to quickly and aggressively develop sports and integrate the country into the global village superstar arena. Sports have to be developed to a level where it will play an active role in Nigerian economy, politics, finances, and society. It would also create millions of jobs.

There is professional soccer leagues in Nigeria, but the quality of the leagues are so poor that fans are not enticed to watch most of the matches. Have Nigerian leaders ever wondered why Nigerians would rather watch other advanced leagues like English premier, Italian league, Spanish league etc. than local Nigerian leagues? Nigeria's idea of soccer is not the same in other countries, because there are just few self-made stars in the country; even the fields the matches were being played look so unkempt and terrible. Advanced leagues have one or two super-stars (actors) that make those matches interesting, not only because of the quality of field and the atmosphere where the matches are being played but also because the players are more skillful and they receive many promotions from the media.

Reduction in Underground World Activities

Most of the men and women that are engaged in the underground economic (bad guys) activities might not have been there, if only other windows of opportunities were available to them. There is no way that every human being must be a respected academician; those that were not gifted in such areas might have been divinely and uniquely packaged with other talents that Nigerian leaders were never interested in developing. "An average human being would rather prefer to be notorious and famous in good than evil, but when good is not available, he settles for evil just to make ends meet" Just like the saying goes "When the desirable is not available, the available becomes the reluctant desirable" Life is a terrible thing to waste.

Many Nigerian armed robbers, kidnappers, hired assassins, militants and drug traffickers would have been in one meaningful sports arena or the other, striving and competing to be the best. When we motivate and encourage good activities, we automatically relegate some devilish activities to the back stage; the country must turn away from chronic corruption and embrace good governance because good governance would increase GDP (gross domestic products) while reducing underground world economy.

Reduction in Secret Cult Activisms in Schools

Reduction in Secret Cult activisms in schools; "Nobody can meaningfully stop a perceived evil in any civil society without providing alternatives to such evil". For anybody to say that there is no high level of secret cult activisms in many higher learning institutions in Nigeria is in denial and might have difficulty finding solutions to such high levels of secret cult activisms. Developing amateur sports should start in early ages and culminate in their final university years when they will be getting ready to turn into professionals. Since all the students are not academically inclined, some of them must be available for inhuman activities by the stakeholders of underground economic activities, because chronic corruption has made the government unable to provide these students with viable alternative to cultism. No child should be left behind, so Nigerian leaders should get back to the drawing board and strategize on the way forward. Nigerian leaders should give these kids many other alternatives to discourage them from joining men of the underground world economy.

If Nigerian leaders can help develop amateur sports in all the higher learning institutions, such sporting events might encourage them not to join secret, violent cult groups. Remember that these children are the future hope of the nation, and if secret cult activism continues to take the better part of their lives, kidnapping, armed robberies, prostitutions, political hooliganism and militancy groups will continue to increase. Can Nigeria be the next global engine of growth without grooming her future leaders and conquering chronic corruption?

Job Creations

Since sports generate over two trillion dollars all over the world, nobody can realistically put a fair number on the sports related jobs that would be created in Nigeria, but it would definitely not be less than five million, considering the population of the country. The question now would be if corruption does not play active role in sports development through the appointment of political personnel that might not be adequately suited for the positions. Nigeria is a wonderful country that God provided everything for, but the high level of corruption has negated the development of all the resources and talents God endowed on the country.

Nigeria definitely has the potential of being the most loved and darling of the global village in terms of investments, if only it can find a way to curb its chronic corruption. Among all the converging countries in the global village, Nigeria is one of the many countries that Mother Nature has showed mercy with reference to weather. God must have seen something in Nigeria that the world has not been able to discover, including Nigerians themselves. Nigerian leaders should not forget that chronic corruption is what brews African life-presidents, briberies, tribal sentiments, religious-divide and inefficiencies in governance of the continent. Until aggressive war is declared and won against chronic corruption, Nigeria and some many other African countries will remain under-developing economies with no clear vision for the future.

There might be a need for new-colonization or re-colonization of Nigeria in the unlikely event that Nigerian leaders are not forthcoming in bringing transparent reforms that will sustain unity of the people and grow political and economic activities in the country. It is so sad to see what is happening in Nigeria today, where the professionals and technocrats have been replaced with political appointees to head strategic positions. How long can Nigerian leaders pilot this big aircraft that is greatly losing altitude at an alarming speed, without crashing the aircraft down the line? Wake up Nigeria; you are the giant of Africa with enough manpower and resources to tower Africa to a respected continent.

Do Nigerian leaders really want to see the crash of Air Nigeria that is yearning for qualified crew members? Once again, Nigerian Leaders must reform or be transformed by the sixth columnist to an unknown end. China and other countries cannot wait any longer to speed up their re-colonization efforts in Nigeria; therefore, Nigerians must make sacrifices and rally around their new administration to pilot Air Nigeria to high and suitable altitude that would shield the aircraft away from those severe turbulences that are capable of crashing the prestigious Air Nigeria. Nigeria, the world loves you, but you must walk away from decades of motivationally configured and systematically encouraged looting of your needed resources to develop your country.

CHAPTER 4

Expanding Nigerian Stock Exchange Market

Nigerian stock exchange has the key to unlock the wealth of the nation through financial engineering that would create surplus capital in the country, but the regulatory authority must level the playing fields that would help to create maximum competition in financial engineering.

The impact of chronic corruption can also be felt on such important institutions because appointments of the executive officers were probably not made to individuals with relative understanding of the global markets. No country can grow to financial maturity without developing the country's stock and commodity market exchanges to a transparent level that would attract sufficient foreign individual and institutional investors. Any nation that is not growing economically should examine the stock market exchanges and make the necessary adjustments for production, because building a solid nation requires financial engineering and cheap capital for growth. No one can build a competitive nation on borrowed funds and hired personnel.

A meaningful economic and financial growth in Nigeria will greatly depend on how much the country is able to develop and expand her Stock Market exchanges. Developed and developing countries were not built on highly borrowed funds, and borrowing to build industries and build infrastructures in Nigeria would definitely not work. If a nation can borrow money in a low single digit, yes the nation can succeed to some extent, but any interest rate charges from high single to double digits percentage cannot sustain any economy. Can you imagine when companies can now get capital at the fractional cost of interest rate charges from the stock exchange market through the issuance of equities like in advanced nations?

Growth of companies in such nations can never be limited, so the Nigerian government has to enable the playing fields for emergency of other smaller stock and commodity exchange to help in creating capital for the growth of companies. Apart from chronic corruption, high interest rates charges in Nigeria are among the destabilizing growth factors in the country. Young, promising manufacturing companies and factories were forced to close out quickly because of high interest rate charges from commercial banks. The benefits of functional Stock Market exchanges in Nigeria cannot be adequately emphasized in this book, but it is very important to highlight some key areas; such as the following:

- Cheap Funds to quoted companies

- Expansion of companies

- Export promotions

- Opportunity for the public wealth accumulation

The easiest and fastest way for companies to grow meaningfully would be to source funds from the domiciled stock exchange market thereby reducing the cost of capital. A reputable or well-managed company can go to a local stock exchange market and raise cheap funds through the issuance of the company's shares. With the advice and guidance of investment bankers, the company can raise millions of dollars through Initial Public Offering (IPO) or through Right issues to existing shareholders at less than a onetime fee of about 8% of the total amount raised.

You can never compare raising money from stock exchanges to borrowing monies from banks to operate companies or industries on a long-term basis, because the difference is clear. At the 17% to 32% interest rates charges that some Nigerian banks charge their good customers, it will be a miracle for any company to survive on such high interest rate charges on long-term basis. Private placements are usually the first steps for any company that wishes to do an Initial Public Offering (IPO) down the line. This is also a wonderful and cheaper way of raising capital for companies that have long term growth strategies. Nigeria as a country can never grow when most of the companies are not creating enough jobs that would give Nigerians disposable incomes.

A company that must survive on high interest rate charges from banks, must enjoy a total monopoly of its niche market and must continue to grow at a sequential yearly rate of thirty-eight (38%) percent. Anything less than the above percentage rate, will see the company being liquidated within four years. If some states can be encouraged and supported by federal government and Nigerian stock exchange to open minor stock exchanges, many more medium and large scale companies in such states can go there and be listed in the local stock exchanges, and might even be cross-listed in the major stock exchanges when they qualify.

Once a company goes public, the rate of the company's growth will elevate to an over-drive, because more investors that bought shares in the company might likely start to patronize such a company. A company's successful outing to the public will translate to the company having so much money to embark on projects that the company deems profitable to the shareholders. The rate of the company's expansion will also quadruple, because people will now get to hear about the company's products and services.

Relating to what happened in Nigeria some years back, when Central Bank of Nigeria (CBN), under the leadership of Professor Charles Soludo, forced Nigerian commercial banks to re-capitalize from their mere Two Billion Naira (N2,000,000,000) to Twenty-five billion (N25,000,000,000) capital base. Amazingly most of these commercial banks went to the Nigerian stock exchange and miraculously raised the needed capital. This incident confirms that there is actually so much money in circulation, but outside the banking sector. For any economy to grow meaningfully too much money does not need to be on the sideline; most of the monies need to be in either the banking system or in the capital markets to help multiply the effect of money supply.

The N25,000,000,000 re-capitalization process also witnessed the era of unprecedented mergers and acquisitions in the banking sector that streamlined the number of commercial banks from almost 90 banks to just 21 banks with better cash reserves. The surviving 21 banks are now much stronger, and have embarked on an extensive branch network throughout Nigeria and other African countries. The recapitalization exercise is actually one of the best things that came out of President Olusegun Obasango's administration from 1999 to 2007. However chronic corruption has eaten up the gains from that commendable bank exercise.

The financial and economic effects of the bank's action were increasingly felt throughout the country because of their big surge on economic activities. Banks that were barely holding their heads above the water, suddenly raised over one thousand percent (1,000%) of whatever amount that held their lifelines in the society. The banks actually went searching for financing and lending activities from the public. However, since the banks cannot go into long-term lending because of unpredictable high inflationary growth rate, they first attacked the Nigerian Stock Exchange market, and once the market got over-bought, the banks rushed to properties; and when the bubble busted in real estate, they went into branch network expansion.

One can clearly see why there is no fundamental and organic growth in the Nigerian economy, because all the money the commercial banks raised from the stock exchange market that was supposed to go to the real sectors never made it to the real sector. The commercial banks still refuse to go into long-term lending because of high inflationary rate that would consume any commercial bank venture into long term lending. The commercial banks cannot grow organically without the elimination of chronic corruption by Nigerian government, because evil begets evil.

Despite all the monies that Nigerian banks raised, the real sector of the economy was still ignored because the banks are concerned about the effect of surging inflation on their loan portfolios. Nigerian banks are still not efficiently and effectively servicing the real sector of economy, because of fear of unpredictable high inflationary growth rate that continues to surge as a result of unabated chronic corruption. Growing Nigerian economy efficiently will definitely require collective efforts and sacrifices from all Nigerians to help the new administration conquer chronic corruption, the political altitude of any nation, would determine the economic height of the nation.

Do Nigerians blame the banks for not going into long-term lending that would help to turn Nigerian economy from import-oriented to export-oriented economy? Are the banks' actions justified for only short-term lending? Yes, to an extent. If Nigerian government has refused to bring down chronic corruption to a manageable level, which will help to checkmate the high inflationary growth rate on the country, then the banks are rightfully justified to make returns to their shareholders.

The banks can only achieve profits by making short-term lending that will guarantee at least the value of their capital when customers return borrowed money back to the banks. This is why Nigerian banks' preferred customers are importers. They try to shy away from manufacturers, unless it is just for short-term lending, because the purchasing power of the nation's currency goes down over 10% annually.

Nigerian government must find ways to help and encourage commercial banks to go into long-term lending; as this is one of the best strategies to build a sustainable and stable economy in the country. Nigerian Apex bank can also set aside large sums of money for manufacturing sectors only, and effectively monitor the disbursements of such funds to the manufacturing sector, or chronic corruption will annex such funds. The funds would be given to commercial banks at not more than 5%, and the commercial banks can lend this amount to manufacturers at not more than 7%.

Nigerians should be given merit awards for their mindsets in always trying to circumvent important policies that were meant to help the country grow. In this case, the government, Apex Bank, and Security & Exchange Commissions should carefully monitor the discounted lending to banks to make sure that the intended recipients (manufacturers) get the money at the assumed low interest rate without many bottlenecks. It is very unfortunate to say that the Nigerian economy is collapse-bound, if the stakeholders cannot bring down interest rate charges to about 13%, which would help the manufacturers to create jobs and organically grow the economy, and put the country on the path to greatness. Politically, economically and financially, Nigerian government might remain unstable until the commercial banks, which are the oxygen of the economy start going into long term lending that would help to grow gainful jobs; the country will remain grossly under-developed.

When companies go public, their appendages also expand drastically thereby creating more awareness nationally. Successful manufacturing companies that went public some few years ago are now repositioning themselves for exporting more of their finished products; which were occasioned by the increase in plant capacity utilization. Suffice it to say, not all the companies that went public must embark on export promotions, but Nigerian informed investors would not mind putting their money in those companies that are engaged in export activities to the Western world; as that will be another form of leverage against the high inflationary growth rate in the country.

Export activities really need to increase in Nigeria to help the country reduce the high volume of pressure that the country's economic style of import-based economy is putting on the currency (Naira). If the country cannot grow her export businesses now that IMF is at the verge of forcing the country to devalue her currency, then the (₦) Naira might be exchanged at a rate of ₦300 to $1 very soon. Falling crude oil price and depleting foreign reserve is a deadly combination that the new administration urgently has to address, because Nigeria really needs more money now to start replacing the decaying infrastructures.

A company that produces enough for export will always have a comparative advantage over its contemporaries that manufacture solely for local consumptions, let Nigerian government encourage the manufacturers to increase their production capacities and export excess inventories. Manufacturing enough for export will also entail a huge capital outlay that can easily be embarked upon when the company increases her financial status by raising money from a local stock exchange at a fractional cost of borrowing from banks, or through private placements.

One of the major advantages of raising money through a stock exchange market is the expansion of the stakeholders' base. The public can now buy and sell common shares of this particular company in the exchange that the company is listed in, for capital gains. Some shareholders definitely would want to patronize the company to help grow their investments too. Depending on how good the company is performing, individual investments in the company can grow faster than the high rate of inflationary growth in the country.

Nigerians should be reminded once again, that the best forms of investments in a highly anticipated inflationary growth rate are stocks and real estate; as such investments would grow to accommodate the high inflation rate. Nonetheless, investing in common stocks is the best way to grow your portfolio when the rate of inflation is so high. Stock prices have ways of adjusting for high inflationary growth rate in any given country. This is the primary reason financial advisers are always quick to recommend buying shares of blue chip companies over buying bonds, certificate of deposits (CDs) or saving accounts. Suffice it to say, investment recommendations will depend on the following:

- Investment time horizon

- Investor's Age

- Investment Objective

- Investor's risk tolerance level

Please remember to always discuss with your financial adviser a recommended portfolio mix that will be suitable for your individual need. Individual investors have different reasons for investing; and as such, their portfolio mix needs to be strategically balanced to meet such objectives.

To really expand and deepen Nigerian stock exchange, Nigerian government through security and exchange commission (SEC) would seriously have to take a second look at establishing regional stock exchanges in some industrial cities and at the same time, embark on promoting the activities of the stock exchanges throughout the country, because there is so much money outside the financial institutions that definitely would help to grow the country's economy. Nigeria and stock exchange stakeholders really have to go beyond the traditional listing of multi-national companies and some other national companies. The extent of industrialization in Nigeria will largely depend on how the Nigerian stock exchange stakeholders and SEC would welcome the new normal which is financial engineering. The country needs to urgently establish regional and commodity exchanges in the major cities to put the country a step towards greatness.

Establishment of Regional Stock Exchanges

The Nigerian banking sector would have crashed and collapsed the entire economy, if not for the fact that the Nigerian Stock Exchange played an active part in helping the banks to re-capitalize to the new bench mark of twenty-five billion Naira capital base. One can imagine what would happen in Nigerian economy if the Nigerian stock exchange remains non-active or too shallow to play an active and leading role in financial engineering. Nigerians must be sensitized on the importance of stock exchanges in nation building and why the country cannot grow meaningfully unless the masses start to invest part of their saving on equities. Nigeria must have some regional stock market exchanges that would help to reach the majority of the masses in the promotion of stock exchanges in the country, because all the developed countries were technically built from cheap capitals sourced from stock exchanges.

Meanwhile, the level at which Nigerian commercial banks raised millions of dollars from the Nigerian Stock Exchanges within a very short period of time was very astronomical, because that shows there is so much money outside the financial institutions. The success might also indicate that there might be too much money in circulation, or more foreign investors have renewed interests in Nigerian economy. Whatever the case may be, Nigerian financial advisers were very happy that all hands were on deck to save the Nigerian banking sector. The question still remains though; how can Nigeria efficiently grow her small, medium and large-scale companies with cheap funds that will help to make them export-oriented companies?

The secret of functionally growing Nigerian economy on a large scale will depend heavily on the establishment of regional stock exchanges, and transparent SEC that would regulate the activities of all the stock exchanges in the country. The Nigerian Stock Exchange, State governments, Commercial banks, Stockbrokers and other high net-worth individual investors need to have round table conferences and devise means of urgently establishing regional stock exchanges in major cities because the projects would create probably 30,000 jobs within a reasonable time frame.

Regional stock exchanges in other relatively developed cities with a high concentration of industrial activities will encourage well-managed small, medium and large-scale companies to go and raise funds through the issuance of penny stocks. There is so much money outside the Nigerian banking system and these regional stock exchanges need to go after these funds; but, commercial banks need this chunk of money outside the banking system to increase M2 supply.

A small, medium and large-scale company with a good and practicable business plan can approach the regional stock exchange in the state where it does business for IPO through penny stocks. Since the company does business in that state, some indigenes of that state might be familiar with the company's products or services and will probably commit some money to this company. In this case, the chances of the company raising funds through IPO is very high, and as such those companies must be invited and encouraged by the regional stock exchanges to come and issue penny stocks to the public.

It will be a wonderful thought-out recommendation if the Nigerian stock exchange invests in all these regional stock exchanges; as Nigerian stock exchange might eventually reach out to the performing darling companies of the regional exchanges and encourage them to be cross-quoted in the big boards (Nigerian major stock exchange) for the benefit of the all Nigerians. Some big companies in America went through the penny stock process popularly known as Over the Counter Bulletin Board (OTC BB). This process must be seen as the oxygen that will ignite and revolutionize Nigerian infant industrialization to a modern height. It is very difficult to innovate with borrowed funds, henceforth invested funds are one of the good innovational tools and Nigerians must be motivationally encouraged to invest in Nigerian stock exchange markets.

The Nigerian Stock Exchange's stringent requirement in protecting investors from fraudsters might be difficult for so many small and medium-scale companies to meet. However, since the risks in the regional stock exchanges are much higher than the Nigerian stock exchange, these companies can go to the regional exchanges that do business and issue penny stocks. The risks in penny stocks are much higher; so are the returns, but they are geared towards this way for the investors that have appetites for higher risks and higher returns.

Benefits of Regional Stock Exchanges: If and when the idea of these regional stock exchanges are fully carried out, the nation, the states and cities in which the regional stock exchanges are located will benefit immensely in the following areas;

1.   Reduction in the nation, states or cities unemployment levels

2.   Boom in the economic activities in the country

3.   Cheap source of capital

1) Reduction in the nation, states or cities unemployment levels

Nigeria, States and cities that successfully establish regional stock exchanges in their areas will witness huge reduction in the high unemployment level in their respective states. Once some companies complete their Initial Public Offerings (IPO) from these regional stock exchanges, the companies will definitely use the raised funds for expansion, and this will mean employing more people from those areas. More and more jobs will be created in those states; and these actions will also translate into more families having disposable income that would come back into the economy again.

2) Boom in the economies of those states

The economic activities of the states that would successfully establish regional exchanges will greatly witness increase economic activities through the availability of cheap capital in such areas. The economic impact of those companies that raised funds from the regional exchanges will be felt in all areas from their surge of spending in the locality. Contractors, skilled and unskilled laborers will be fully engaged in the expansion phases of these companies made possible by cheap capital. high rates of crime and other fraudulent activities will drastically decrease also.

3) The cheap source of capital

This is one of the mitigating factors holding Nigeria back from marching into greatness—cheap source and availability of capital. Companies that operate in areas where there are regional stock exchanges will definitely enjoy more robust growth as the regional stock exchanges will come in handy for cheap capital and other growth ideas. Companies find it very difficult to meaningfully grow with the high interest rates that Nigerian banks charge to manufacturing companies and that explains why importing businesses flourish more than local producing businesses, because commercial banks can only provide short term loans.

Once again, it is okay to reiterate the importance of establishing these regional stock exchanges, because it will be an illusion if Nigeria is bent on building functional, viable, and sustainable economy on borrowed funds and labor. Building Nigerian economy to a level that would attract global accolades must be a collective team effort of creating rooms for cheap capital, and that is the major reason the investing public should be motivated, configured and encouraged to patronize the regional stock exchanges, while the government will make sure that those individuals trying to take undue advantage of the exchanges would be severely punished accordingly.

Suffice it to say, that there would not be any competition between the Nigeria Stock Exchange and the regional Stock Exchanges, because they both will be playing in different leagues under the watchful eyes of the Security and Exchange Commission (S.E.C). The major and minor regional stock exchanges really have to co-exist in order to promote innovation and fundamental growth in the Nigerian economy. Establishing more stock exchanges in the country would bring about financial engineering, and without financial engineering that would create cheap and excess capital liquidity in Nigeria. The country might definitely be slow in attending greatness because fame and greatness requires innovation, creativity, reforms, rule of law, functional government systems, resilience and the tenacity of majority of the masses to succeed.

There should be clearly defined tasks between the Nigerian stock exchanges and the regional stock exchanges to avoid any unwarranted and unhealthy competitions among the exchanges. In line with the arguments of adding towns and villages in the power sharing formula in the country, the regional stock exchanges would help the towns to create wealth that would sustain the inhabitants of the towns and villages. At the same time, the regional stock exchanges would help to bring innovation and financial engineering to the local companies, while the Nigerian Stock Exchange will carter to the needs of national and global companies that meet the exchange-listing requirements. Come to think of it, the regional exchanges will help to deepen the Nigerian stock exchange by creating more awareness for the investing public; and companies that might be working hard to be quoted on Nigeria stock exchange will have to maintain a performance trend record.

Regional stock exchanges could eventually prove to be relatively quality investments for banks that get actively involved in the setting up of these stock exchanges. When referring to said quality investments, it is like saying that the banks will be investing in projects that can even rescue the banks when there is a serious liquidity crunch in the country. Nigerian fixed income market will also come to limelight when the empowered towns and villages would now approach the regional stock exchanges for listing of their municipal bonds.

Another government establishment that must be encouraged to be independently powerful is the Security and Exchange Commission (S.E.C), because it would help to purge insider-traders (investors taking advantage of material non-public information) and attract both retail and foreign investors. If the SEC is not independent and powerful, then Nigerian dreams of having viable emerging market status would be a far-fetched program because transparency will be lacking in the stock exchanges. An independently powerful S.E.C will help to speed up the establishment of other exchanges like Regional Stock Exchanges, Commodity Exchanges, and Options Exchanges, Corporate and public bond exchanges.

A nation like Nigeria needs all or most of the above mentioned exchanges to elevate financial engineering to a level that would create excess liquidity for annual GDP double digits growth for many years. Once again, no group of people can build a great nation with borrowed money and labor. Nigeria really needs to create common interest and financial engineering through the stock exchanges and unity through sports. Technology has made it easy to set up a stock market exchange with a fraction of what it used to be, and Nigeria should be taking advantage of the technological breakthrough.

Recommendations

In order to make the Security and Exchange Commission (S.E.C) independently powerful, the governments should immediately set up a board, comprised of financial-oriented individuals from both within and outside the country. The mandate should be with a minimum of sixty days (60) to review all the existing laws that established the S.E.C in Nigeria and to determine if any modification is necessary in making these establishments viably and independently powerful to regulate all the Exchanges. In addition to reviewing existing laws, there might also be a serious need to address the following issues;

1. That Nigerian Security and Exchange Commission (S.E.C) will consists of seven people appointed by the President with the advice and consent of the Senate.

2. That all S.E.C Commissioners are appointed for six-year terms to outlive any president that appoints them.

3. The Commissioners may have no other businesses or employments other than this job.

4. The six-year terms will be staggered so that a new Commissioner will be appointed by every president that spends 8 years in office.

5. To minimize the level of political shenanigans, the Commissioners will be drawn from the ruling parties, opposition parties, and other economists from the private sector.

6. Because of the sensitive nature of the job, all S.E.C Commissioners may not be allowed to engage in any personal securities transactions. All securities positions they had when they were appointed must be placed into blind trust.

7. The Commissioners must comprise of people with good global capital market, financial and economic knowledge to help them in articulating viable and meaningful regulatory policies.

8. A good incentive package should be given to a whistle blower that leads to recovery of money from insider trades.

The Security and Exchange Commission must be willing and ready for their new roles to regulate and promote Nigerian Stock Exchanges which would make the exchanges more transparent and also the darling of all foreign, institutional and retail investors. More and more funds need to start heading into Nigeria in the form of investments, but without transparency of Security and Exchange Commission, such wishful expectations might not come to fruition. The SEC must be the catalyst that will ignite such a move that would create the level of financial engineering that would provide cheap excess funds in the country.

This is a choice that the new administration has to quickly make to move Nigeria into the league of global financial power houses. Nigeria has resources, but qualified personnel must be harnessed in other to effectively and efficiently galvanize these resources into fruitfulness. The Nigerian government must shy away from appointing politicians and their friends into certain strategic positions like Central Bank of Nigeria (CBN) Governor and Security and Exchange Commission (SEC) Chairman because the growth of the country is intertwined with the activities of these establishments. The positions are so vital especially the CBN governor because the wrong choice definitely destroys the national long term growth prospect. The first choice of any CBN governor must include an economist with global overview and ability to work with a team of experts from different professions. The Nigerian government has made so many poor choices in the past with regards to appointments of non-economists to the strategic positions like CBN and other key positions that are vital in the growth of the country.

The major primary objective of security and exchange commission will be to seek out all the institutional and individual insider traders, and use some of them as escape-goats. The first group of insider traders must be made to face well-publicized court trials before being sentenced to a minimum of 10 years in prison. Make no mistake, the public court trials will create public awareness of the consequences of insider trading crimes and at the same time increase the number of retail investors seeking to get into Nigerian Stock Exchanges, because the equity market can never be deepened without the participation of retail investors. The whistle-blower that leads to any arrest of any insider trader must receive 5%-10% of any recovered funds, as this incentive will make others start blowing the whistle for better and transparent Nigerian stock exchanges.

Nigeria needs a vibrant and transparent stock exchange market to be able to attract institutional and retail foreign investors that would help to create liquidity in our equity markets. Once again, Nigerian innovations will be very difficult without transparent stock exchange markets that would compete in financial engineering products that would envelop the country with cheap and excess funds for meaningful national growth. Financial regulatory transparency will definitely beget increased capital inflow that would help to encourage technical and financial innovations that are vital to national growth.

There are other products that the Nigerian stock exchange market really needs to consider bringing into the market, because such products like Short sales, Margins and Options would help to create volatility and deepen the stock exchange market.

Short sales

This is a creative way of using dormant and non-performing share certificates to make money with individuals and institutional investors that are willing to take risks. Individual and Institutional investors are allowed to borrow and sell shares in anticipation of buying those share certificates back at later time from sock brokerage firms. The stock brokerage firms would charge the risk takers (investors/speculators) few amounts for borrowing the certificates and when they buy back the sold certificates, they will keep any profit or loss made from such transactions. Can you imagine if Mr. John goes to any commercial bank with a deposit of ₦10,000,000 Naira into his account, and the bank said to the staff, do not touch the money, just leave it and any time Mr. John comes for his money we will give it to him? How can the commercial banks grow and help the economy of the country, if the banks are not allowed to lend peoples deposits out to individuals that are willing to take risks? The same is applicable to share certificates, institutional and retail investors that are willing to take calculated risks.

This is actually part of the reasons why Nigerian stock market exchange remains shallow and unattractive to many foreign institutional and retail investors. Let the stakeholders quickly introduce short sales into the market and see the level of growth that would be witnessed within short period of time. The author would be more than glad to volunteer his time to help educate stockbrokers and institutional investors on how to profit with short sales.

Margin Account

This is another creative way of enlarging and deepening the Nigerian stock market exchange because individual and institutional investors are also allowed to borrow a certain percentage amount to buy shares into their trading accounts. For example, an individual or institutional can buy 10,000,000 Naira worth of First or Zenith bank shares pay only 1,000,000 to the stock brokerage firm, while the stock brokerage firm will put down the 9,000,000 (maybe borrowed from commercial bank) difference. There are also fees that are associated in using margin accounts to purchase shares. Nigerians can now see how the daily transaction volumes will be increase and at the same time attracting more foreign institutional and individual investors.

Options

Options are form of derivatives that represent contracts sold by one party who wrote the options to another party who bought the option. The contracts offer the buyers the rights, but not the obligation, to buy (call) or sell (put) a security or other financial asset at an agreed-upon price (**the strike price**) during a certain period of time or on a **specific date** (exercise date). Call options give buyers the option to buy at certain price, so the buyer would want the stock price to go up above the strike price stipulated in the contracts. Put options give buyers the option to sell at a certain price, so the buyer would want the stock price to go down below the strike price. In America all monthly options will expire on the third Friday of every month. Here is how option works;

Let us assume that on April 30, 2015, the price of Zenith Bank share is ₦50 for 1, and if Mr. John thinks that the Zenith bank share price will be heading to ₦80 in 5 months, he wants to buy 10,000 shares of Zenith Bank. Therefore, he will have to pay ₦50 * 10,000 = ₦500,000 but John doesn't want to commit that amount for the purchase. He can go and buy 100 Call Option Contracts (one unit option contract holds 100 shares of the equity) for the right to purchase 10,000 shares of Zenith bank in September 2015, so John might see a call option contract like this, Zenith 60 Sept18 2015 selling for N2 each. Meaning 1 call option of Zenith at ₦60 in September 18th 2015 For John to buy this call option contract, it will cost him (2*100 * 100= ₦20, 000) to own 10,000 shares of Zenith bank until September 18th 2015 expiration day. As the underlying equity that has the option goes up, so would the price of the call option contracts will be going up too. If at the end of September 18th 2015 Zenith bank share sells for N75 per share, John can exercise the call option by buying 10,000 units of Zenith bank shares paying only ₦600, 000 which will give John a profit of (₦75*10,000 =₦750,000) current value – his purchasing costs of (₦20, 000 contract fees plus 600,000 purchase price of 10,000 shares)

His profit will be ₦750, 000 – ₦620,000 = **₦130, 000 profit in 5 months.** Now if at the end of September 18th 2015 Zenith bank is selling at N59 per share, John will now let the call option contract expire and his loss will be N₦20, 000 only. Supposing that John bought 10,000 shares of Zenith bank at N50 on April 30th 2015 he would have paid ₦500,000 to own those shares and at a current price of ₦59 per share, he will be making 59 * 10,000 = ₦590,000 – ₦500,000 = ₦90,000 only. The individual and institutional investors just have to calculate the risks that are involved in option trading.

CHAPTER 5

Nigerian Commercial Banks

The roles of banks in any nation can never be adequately addressed in this book, because banks are the heartbeat of any economy. Just like the roles of hospitals are very critical in saving human lives in a nation, banks roles are also critical in keeping the economy of any nation functional. A nation ought to be saved first before saving the lives of the citizens, if life must be enjoyed. What good is it to a man if the banks are failing in his country, and he cannot find a job that will help him sustain the financial needs of his family? All professions are very vital in our everyday existence, but some professions are highly placed above others, and those professions really need to be readily available.

From Bankers that keeps the economy buoyant to Doctors/Nurses that save and maintain lives, to Teachers that impact knowledge to the citizens and to the laborers that keep our environment clean; these professions are all intertwined to help mankind enjoy a better life. Huge shortage of any of the professions will definitely create scarcity of labor and will make the fees we pay for such services very exorbitant or even unaffordable to the majority of people. Abundance of any profession on the other hand will cause supply-overflow and result in demand destruction that will force peanut pay for such services. That is why it is good to maintain equilibrium in all goods and services.

Citizens of all nations are very important; from the president that calls the shots, to prostitutes that solves the sexual needs of some men (reducing cases of rape), to criminals that help to create jobs for security officers & guards, to murderers that helps to remind the citizens of evil in the society. We are all intertwined together and any profession that is lacking in any country will definitely present dysfunctional issues and economic imbalance. A nation is a sub-ecosystem in our global village ecosystem. Any nation that is not functional would definitely have some problems trying to plug into the main ecosystem of the world.

Banks are capable of making or destroying any economy and as such, the banks should be well regulated to make sure that the banker's work within the set rules and regulations that makes banking seamless and efficient. Failure to adequately regulate the banks might result in financial crisis that are capable of causing social, financial and economic problems for the nation. The Central Banks of Nigeria should be well equipped with Economists, Bankers, Stockbrokers, Attorneys, and other professions that would help to formulate monetary policies for the country and at the same time regulate commercial banks, and other financial institutions.

There is a financial imbalance in a country like Nigeria, where the banking sector is the only performing sector. It simply means that other sectors are definitely lacking the necessary liquidity for growth. In the case of Nigerian non-productiveness, chronic corruption and surging underground economy are constantly making it impossible for the banks to go into long term lending, which helps the banks to successfully reposition the country's business style into import-oriented economy.

Nigerian banks need to play active roles in creating level playing fields for the growth of the country's economy, or the country will never bring out her millions of unemployed youths from the labor market. The Nigerian government's inability to control high inflationary growth rates brought about by chronic corruption in the country, has forced most commercial banks to shy away from long-term lending, thereby turning the economy into import-oriented economy that is not suitable for job creation. As a result of commercial banks not going into long-term lending, Nigerian economy is now growing in-organically, and this is a dangerous trend which must be bunged immediately.

It is incredibly sad that some commercial banks are currently charging over 30% to lend money to the main street, while the federal government watches helplessly as unemployment rate among youths escalates, and manufacturing companies are folding up due to high cost of production and unavailability of capital. You cannot build any nation with borrowed funds and high interest rate charges to the nation builders. Financial engineering must be made to be the new normal in the country. Financial engineering would help to address seed capital and long term project needs in the country, while banks will have excess funds to lend out at reduced charges to sectors that are looking for short term working capital.

Nigeria is running an import-oriented economy that is not adequately suited for effective and efficient job creation in any system of economy. Moreover, due to chronic corruption in the country, Nigerian under-ground economy is now growing faster than the real economy because of federal governments' inability to combat high inflationary growth rate. Corruption is malevolence, because it breeds the likes of bribery, high growth rate in under-ground economy, high inflationary rate, armed robberies, absolute political and economic manipulative powers, high unemployment rates, and crime rates. How long can Nigeria survive without killing chronic corruption and embark on innovation and transparent reforms?

The roles of banks in growing any economy are very vital because banks are the heartbeats of any nation. Nigerian Central bank has to wake-up to this high inflationary growth rate challenges, as this will help Nigerian commercial banks to go back into the ethics of banking and long-term lending that will help to meaningfully, fundamentally, technically and organically grow the country's economy. Nigerian currency is quickly losing its purchasing power on double-digit margins annually and if Nigerians cannot be encouraged to start becoming productive, the nation's currency Naira might be heading to ₦300 to $1 in not too distant time. The currency is also losing its exchange rate value against other major currencies of the world. Why? All because of high growth rate of corruption that is fast changing how businesses are being done in Nigeria. Like the new president Muhammadu Buhari rightly said "chronic corruption is even worse than terrorism" The president was absolutely right because chronic corruption has wreaked havoc in the country and at the same time, threatening the fabric that held the ethnic groups together.

In Nigerian capital market today, the most viable and energetic sector for institutional and retail investors is the banking sector, indicating that there are more sinister baskets of problems in the country's economy. The Nigerian banking sector is the primary sector that has shown consistency in growth for the past decades. It accounts for over seventy percent (70%) in terms of both volumes and values in Nigerian nascent stock exchanges. This is really wrong, but until government fiscal and monetary policies help to meaningfully grow the economy to a sustainable level, the banks will only remain the viable sector to invest money in Nigeria.

Meanwhile, other sectors are still struggling to hold their heads above the water; and the same is true in the real estate sector, as bulks of the employment are from the same banking sector. This simply means that the Nigerian economy is not growing organically and if the masses fail to support the new administration to conquer chronic corruption, then the country would remain in vicious cycle, where the ugly past is likely to repeat. Since the only visible growth is in the sector that was supposed to service the entire economy, then the country is in deeper trouble than Nigerians themselves can comprehend.

The Nigerian commercial banks need to go back to the ethics of banking to facilitate and kick-drive real economic growth in all other sectors of the country's economy. Banks are very vital in any country because they can make or mar the economy; regrettably so. The Nigerian government made it possible for the commercial banks to mar the country's economy by shying away from the ethics of banking. Some commercial banks in Nigeria today are simply traders because they just extend facilities to importers, and when the goods arrive, will go to the importers warehouses help sell the goods and collect their money immediately.

Until the Nigerian government can aggressively bring down high level of corruption, which will reduce the high rate of inflationary growth to a manageable level, commercial banks cannot go into long-term lending that will wipe away the dysfunctional ties in the Nigerian economy. It is like Nigeria is one of the places in the global village that is not feeling the impending intense heat of the financial meltdown. As soon as Nigerian banks are encouraged and motivated to go into long-term lending in the country, millions of jobs will be available through the establishment of factories that can absolve millions of Nigerian labor force that have saturated the unemployment numbers.

How can Nigerian commercial banks be continuously making so much profit, and yet the banks are willing to pay individual investors over 15% on fixed deposits. We might be looking at a disguised seriously distressed Nigerian banking sector that needs immediate help from the CBN and IMF. The commercial banks actually tied the hands of federal government and CBN because they are still reporting so much quarterly profits, thereby making it impossible for the nation to prepare for the impending financial meltdown in the country. Nigerians are still busy arguing that the impact of the world's financial melt-down will not be felt in the country because the nation is a cash base system. The wasteful nature of Nigerian political systems and the looming demand destruction in crude oil use will definitely create the worst economic and financial nightmare that might force the country to urgently embrace reforms that would help the country to become the next engine of global growth. Nigerian leaders must prepare for the deadliest austerity measure that would soon envelope the country, unless the new administration would be willing to implement some of the recommendations that would help to ameliorate the masses sufferings.

It is true that the Nigerian economic system is cash-based, and that is why Nigerian economy is not growing organically, because a credit system has a bigger multiplication effect on any nation's currency and economic growth. Remember that commercial banks manufacture money when they let the real sectors borrow money on a long term basis, and since Nigerian economy is a cash-based system, it is obvious that Nigerian economy with little credit has limited potential for growth that would absorb the surging birth rate in the country.

The Central Bank of Nigeria compelled all the commercial banks in the country to re-capitalize their capital base some years ago, and at the end of the excise, the commercial banks became liquid and started servicing other sectors again. The country also witnessed high levels of synergy as unprecedented number of mergers and acquisitions that streamlined the number of commercial banks took place. The gains from the bank recapitalization exercise in Nigeria was however short-lived, because the Nigerian government could not bring down the high rate of inflation that would have made the banks go into long-term lending. As a result of government failure to curb the high rate of inflation, the banks went back to their business as usual that turned Nigerian economy into import-oriented one.

Needless to say that the commercial banks must be compelled to shore up their capital base again because of the falling crude price and depleted foreign cash reserve. The sad and bitter feelings that retail investors witnessed during the last recapitalization exercise need to be urgently addressed to position the commercial banks for patronage in the next exercise. Many retail investors that subscribed to banks shares never got the subscribed shares nor their hard earned money back till many years later when the value of the shares are worthless than the subscribed prices. Strong SEC chairman and regional stock exchanges might definitely help to prevent such future occurrences.

The existence of high interest rate charges (19% to 40%) in Nigeria might imply that liquidity is still scare, and that explains why banks are willing to pay as much as 15% for federal funds short-term loans. Can you image how much interest rate Nigerian banks charge to lend money to their best customers? Companies simply work for banks in Nigeria, and that is one of the reasons the cost of productions are much higher than importing the same product from outside the shores of the country.

However, the inability of the Central bank of Nigeria to curtail the high rate of inflationary growth has deterred the commercial banks from the targeted long-term lending. Opinions are still very high that Nigerian Central bank could lower the high inflationary growth rate to a manageable level, if only the government can fight the underground economies more aggressively through crack downs in chronic corruption, and meaningful reforms. Can one imagine CBN governor trying to mop up two hundred billion Naira (200,000,000,000) from the Nigerian economy to cut down inflationary rates, while unknowingly to him that (300,000,000,000) from the underground economy is coming into the system? What do you think would happen in the CBN monetary policy?

The best way for the Nigerian government to have meaningful impact on winning the war against the high inflationary growth rate and the surging underground economy will be to attack chronic corruption from all corners. The Nigerian government must confront chronic corruption head-on to remain relevant in the new one world order, or ignore chronic corruption and be shortly reduced to nothing. The earlier Nigerians confront chronic corruption, the sooner the country will be on the path to meaningfully grow into greatness, and become the next engine of global growth. Assuredly there is corruption in every corner of our global village, Nigeria and other African countries simply failed to put system of check and balances to help suppress corruption from turning into chronic in the country Today, Nigeria is one of the proud leaders in corrupt activities that would not let any gainful projects to develop in the country.

Henceforth, one would like to witness further induced consolidations in the Nigerian commercial banking sector that will bring in the more desired synergy in the banking sector. Meanwhile, the commercial banks can channel more funds into real estate developments, as that sector is yearning for growth. Why wouldn't all the commercial banks in Nigeria start lending money to real estate developers instead of embarking on branch network expansions? The commercial banks cannot lend money long-term because of high inflationary growth rate in the country. Inflation will eat up any commercial bank that will otherwise lend long-term to any sector on 20% or less interest rate charges. Until Nigeria starts winning the numerous wars on chronic corruption, commercial banks will definitely find it very difficult to go into long-term lending because of high inflation rates that constantly devalues the nation's currency.

Chronic corruption begets high inflationary growth rate in any nation and will make the currency of such country to constantly lose purchasing power and exchange rate value faster against other major currencies. All hands must be on deck regardless of your political affiliations, because Nigerians must wrestle their beloved country away from decades of chronic corruption stronghold. It definitely would not be an easy task to reclaim the country, but with enough sacrifices, in no distant time, Nigerians will be on a path of greatness again.

What will be the net effect of the extensive commercial banks surge in building more branches? The impact of the commercial banks' aggressive branch network expansion will turn out to be a negative one to the economy in no distant future, because the marginal returns from some of the branches might not be enough to offset the gains from other branches. The marginal increment from these branches might look good in the balance sheet of these commercial banks initially, but in reality, the branches would constitute losses to these banks because of the increasing operating costs and decreasing customers' base.

The initial objective of Central Bank of Nigeria for increasing the level of liquidity in the banking sector was to kick-start an economic expansionary period that will provide gainful and meaningful employment to the high number of the Nigerian labor force. Agreed that the Apex bank recapitalization policy was a wonderful economic idea, but has it addressed the real economic issue on ground? Nonetheless, the only problem is that no sane commercial bank can go into long-term lending in Nigeria today and remain in business in the near future, because the commercial banks must hedge against the unpredictable high inflationary growth rate in the country. It looks like Nigerian commercial banks are also the victims of prevalent chronic corruption in the country that was rightfully denied the opportunity in helping to build the country. The Nigerian commercial banks were in a nutshell, discouraged by the government from going into long-term lending thereby suffocating the existing industries.

Should commercial banks be blamed for not lending to the real sectors? Absolutely not, because the commercial banks are in the business of making returns to their numerous shareholders and as such want to make profit and hedge against inflation. As it is in Nigeria today, the only major economic expansion will continue to be the commercial banks' expansion of their branches, just to shore-up their assets base, which might be a good hedge against the high inflationary growth rate in the country. It is very difficult in these modern days to grow any economy without adequate if not excess capital at very low interest rate charges. Remember that the panacea to Nigerian path to greatness will depend on the killing of chronic corruption, growth of the stock exchange markets and the level of financial engineering that would take place in the country.

Are Nigerian real sectors and Main Street participating in any economic growth in the country? Is the Nigerian economy functional and productive? The answers to the above questions are unfortunately and sadly no, because the Nigerian economy is dysfunctional because of chronic corruption, and inorganically operating without any contribution from the real sectors.

Unfortunately, the real sectors and Main Street cannot participate in the Nigerian dysfunctional economy, because commercial banks that are holding their life-lines are not giving them enough oxygen that would make them grow and prosper.

Consequently, not until the high inflationary growth rate in Nigeria is down to predictable levels for planning, commercial banks will not be in a hurry to go into long-term lending because no commercial bank would want to give out strong Naira currency and then receive back a highly depreciated and devalued currency. The Nigerian government must fight chronic corruption head-on, bring down high inflationary growth rate, then watch and see how the economy will blossom.

Considering the population of Nigeria at about one hundred and seventy million (170,000,000), the real estate sector is a potential growth sector that might eventually tower Nigerian economy with a real GDP growth. Real estate is a sector that Central Banks of Nigeria must urgently dialogue with commercial banks, and other private sectors to come up with attractive packages that will make it imperative for other sectors to grow. The Real estate sector will help to create millions of jobs, and at the same time streams of incomes to individuals and commercial banks that will help to maintain the sector through monthly mortgage payments. The Nigerian government has been spending billions of unjustified dollars on an agricultural sector that is not known as the superlative tool for massive job creation. Why? The global number of people employed in the agricultural sector has constantly being going down since the turn of the centuries because of advanced technologies that has given mankind farming tractors, planting & harvesting equipment, and other equipment that have displaced millions of people that use to work in the sector. Robots in no distant time might also be put in use to further take away more of the jobs from human beings, the unintended consequences of advance technology is that foods produced by non-humans are definitely cheaper than humans can produce.

Real growth in the real estate sector will skyrocket the gross domestic product (GDP) of Nigeria to a level that will attract foreign institutional investors. The issues still remain, on how the commercial banks can afford to finance homebuyer's desired interest rate of 5% to 7% in an economy whose inflation growth rate might be close to

15%? Everyone really would love to see how this could be achieved without first bringing down chronic corruption to a manageable level.

Another good development in Nigerian banking sector was the growth in inter-regional and intra-country banking that is still growing like wild fire throughout the continent. The unintended consequences of such growth might be the quick failure of commercial banks in the continent, once there is major financial crunch in a country like Nigeria (African big brother).Nigerian commercial banks are in the forefront of this inter-regional banking, because the commercial banks had excess capital from the recapitalization exercise that needed to be invested judiciously for relatively good investment returns to bank's shareholders. Nigerian commercial banks are still spreading out to other African countries, without adequate contagion measures for bank's failures in other parts of Africa. It might be better if these commercial banks spread out to other continents to fully hedge against the high inflationary growth rate in Africa and the impending austerity measures that could lead to more currency devaluations in Africa. Diversification is the new normal for investment in our global village today, so the commercial banks should not conform only in Africa. Spending billions of dollars on agricultural sector is not a sound economic diversification because technology has eaten the mass jobs that agricultural sector used to provide in the 18th century, and banking on human labor to produce foods would make the imported foods cheaper than home grown foods.

Intra/inter country and regional banking are parts of the monumental developments that will help to smooth the progress of the much desired trades between African countries. This is also a good example of one of the benefits from that forced re-capitalization exercise of Nigerian commercial banks by the Central Bank of Nigeria. Can commercial banks that do not have enough capital for their local markets dream of going to establish in other African countries? Thanks to the recapitalization exercise and frankly speaking, Nigerian banks are really due for another round of force recapitalization exercise by the CBN governor. Many more African countries ought to encourage their commercial banks to re-capitalize for the benefits of not just the countries, but the continent.

It is imperative to once again reiterate the significance of long-term lending by Nigerian commercial banks because; it will help to create gainful employments in Nigeria and level the field for technology innovation to some extent. Real growth in Nigerian GDP would be dependent on how much Nigerian government can aggressively bring down the high inflationary growth rate to a manageable level, which will encourage Nigerian commercial banks to go into long-term lending, and give the country a functional economy. The fixed income market is no longer an attractive form of investment for knowledgeable and well informed investors, except where there are no other investment options, as the global village transit from low cost money to rising interest rate charges. Expect the cost of money to start rising up unabated once American federal reserve starts to increase the fed fund rates.

Thousands of graduates are coming out every year in Nigeria to join the already saturated labor market, and it might not be an overstatement to say that Nigerian unemployment rate is one of the highest in the global village because of chronic corruption. Nigerian commercial banks prefer to give facilities to importers rather than manufacturers, all because of high inflationary growth rate. Once again, should we blame the commercial banks for making profits at the expense of Nigerian economy? Not really, because the government has collectively failed to bring down the high inflationary growth rate to an acceptable level, that would have encouraged the banks to go into long term lending.

Nigerian economy can never survive on short term lending; such banking style can only continue to grow the nation's importation business at the expense of the Naira. More emphasis should be centered on bringing down the borrowing costs and long term lending if the country desires to be the next engine of global growth. It is sad when economic advisors of outgoing president Goodluck Jonathan argue that the economy is being diversified because billions of dollars were being spent on the agricultural sector. First, they should have warned him that the level of chronic corruption in the country will automatically kill the efforts in bringing up the agricultural sector, and secondly real diversification would have come from spending such billions on small and medium scale industries and promoting exports at the same time.

Nonetheless, there are many people who are very optimistic that Nigerian commercial banks should go into long-term lending as soon as the government is able to bring down the high inflationary growth rate into manageable level. Meanwhile, millions of Nigerians on the labor market would have to wait for more years, before they could be gainfully employed, because recipients of commercial banks short term lending (importers) cannot create meaningful jobs that will pull out millions of the unemployed Nigerians from the labor market. Suffice it to say that aggregate industrial capacity utilization in Nigeria is running at below forty-eight percent (48%) due to lack of capital while the political class is squandering billions of dollars outside the country.

The helplessness and hopelessness of Nigerian government to motivationally configure the private sector to create jobs could well explain why armed-robberies and other crimes have been on annually frightening increase. Private sector, especially the small and medium scale industries, has to create more jobs; but unfortunately, small and medium scale industries are difficult to survive in Nigeria because of high operating costs and very expensive cost of funds. Cost of capital is very expensive in Nigeria. You hear instances where banks charge up to 40%. Can any company realistically survive on such an interest rate charge? The answer is unequivocally "No" because no individual can build or grow a successful business on such exorbitant interest charges.

Some of the armed robbers in Nigeria today are graduates that could not wait any longer in the labor market. Nigerian government and the commercial banks have collectively failed the poor masses, and unless something very drastic is done to address the problems, the country might be sitting on a keg of very powerful and explosive gun powder capable of blowing away all the ethnic groups in the country. The Nigerian government and the commercial banks must go back to their drawing boards, and come up with employment creating strategies, before the government loses frightening numbers of those in the labor market to men of the under-ground world economy, because the agricultural sector that the government is bragging about cannot create enough jobs as technological breakthroughs and robots are taking over most of the available jobs in the sector.

The Nigerian government must encourage commercial banks to play active roles in a dream Nigeria by bringing down the high rate of inflationary growth rate in the country. Nigerians dream of a country that would equitably re-distribute wealth and bring out over eighty percent (80%) of Nigerians (who are living below the minimum internationally acceptable poverty level), out of poverty might just be a wishful thought. Desired is a Nigeria that will constantly create jobs to reduce high number of criminal activities and move forward the country few steps towards being the next global engine of growth.

A dream Nigeria that will dialogue and create an environment that will wipe away inter-tribal wars, militant groups, kidnappers, armed robbers and deadly student cultism. A country that will put in place checks and balances in all spheres of government to help prevent chronic corruption and check political excess wastes. There will be no gainful and meaningful growth in Nigeria until the government drastically reduces the high level of corruption; then innovations, researches and inventions will start taking place again in the country. Eradicating chronic corruption would eliminate half of the country's major setbacks because most of the country's problems revolve around chronic corruption.

The Nigerian government, CBN, commercial banks and the private sector must collectively and aggressively fight the high inflationary growth rate that is threatening to negate economic gains that Nigeria had accomplished in the past. The high inflationary growth rate in Nigeria is a battle that must be won to save Nigeria from a gloomy and hopeless economic future. It is about time that Nigeria starts fighting chronic corruption more aggressively, because it kills more people than AIDS and terrorists. Millions of people are dying enmasse in Nigeria today, because of malnutrition and starvation that has been orchestrated by chronic corruption that is eroding the purchasing power of Nigerian currency. This might sound so ridiculous but Nigerian currency was valued more than American dollar and British pound in the late seventies and the eighties. In 1981 to be precise, one Naira (Nigerian currency) will get $2 American dollars, and also one Naira will get 1.5 British pounds. Today in Nigeria, it will take you a whopping: 200 Naira to get $1 American. 350 Naira to get 1 British pound.

Nigerian current currency value against the American dollar actually means that inflation in Nigeria has grown over 16,000,000%, in less than forty five years (45). If this whopping rate of inflationary massacre of Nigerian currency goes un-checked, it will take about

1,000 Naira to get 1 American dollar and about 1,500 Naira to get 1 British pound before the year 2030. Nigerian currency devaluation against other major currencies has been aggressively on the wrong trajectory, because Nigerians are not productive and are not willing to combat chronic corruption head-on. The un-commendable Nigerian currency performance must be urgently addressed with a high degree of priority, or Nigeria might run into deadly hard times in the coming years that will likely test once again the pillars of foundations that held the converging ethnic groups together. There might be more civil disobediences and bloody mass demonstrations for change and liberation of the poor masses, if the new administration fails to salvage the country. Failure should not be an option with the new administration because the unintended consequences would definitely rattle the global village.

True reforms in Nigeria are no longer the questions of if, but when and how these reforms should be carried out. The sooner Nigerians can embark on such reforms, will determine where Nigeria will be placed in the global village in coming years. In the unlikely events that Nigerians still refuse to reform genuinely, then the global village might be witnessing re-colonization or new colonization of Nigeria sooner than later by, for instance China. Please take a look at a speech delivered by the then American Secretary of State- Hilary Clinton in June of 2011; incidentally, she has declared her intention as regards of 2016 presidential election in America;

Hillary Clinton Warns Africa of 'New Colonialism'– Reports

11 June 2011 written by Republic Report New York

New York [RR] LUSAKA, Zambia — U.S. Secretary of State Hillary Rodham Clinton on Saturday warned Africa of a creeping "new colonialism" from foreign investors and governments interested only in extracting the continent's natural resources to enrich themselves and not the African people.

Clinton said that African leaders must ensure that foreign projects are sustainable and benefit all their citizens, not only elites. A day earlier, she cautioned that China's massive investments and business interests in Africa need to be closely watched so that the African people are not taken advantage of.

"It is easy, and we saw that during colonial times, it is easy to come in, take out natural resources, pay off leaders and leave," Clinton said. "And when you leave, you don't leave much behind for the people who are there. We don't want to see a new colonialism in Africa." Clinton said the United States didn't want foreign governments and investors to fail in Africa, but they should also give back to the local communities.

"We want them to do well, but also we want them to do good," she said.

"We don't want them to undermine good governance, we don't want them to basically deal with just the top elites, and frankly too often pay for their concessions or their opportunities to invest." Clinton said that American development aid and infrastructure projects come with good governance conditions and that the Obama administration is interested in Africa and the African people.

Their success, she said, is in the long-term interest of both the African people and the U.S. She spoke in a pan-African television interview in the Zambian capital. Her interview followed the handover of a U.S. built pediatric hospital in Lusaka to the Zambian government. Earlier, at the inaugural meeting of the U.S.-Zambia Chamber of Commerce, Clinton laid out the U.S. strategy for helping Africa.

"We want a relationship of partnership not patronage, of sustainability, not quick fixes," she said. "We want to establish a strong foundation to attract new investments; open new businesses … create more paychecks, and do so within the context of a positive ethic of corporate responsibility."

"We think it's essential that we have an idea going in that doing well is not in any way a contradiction of doing good," she said. Clinton is the first secretary of state to visit Zambia since Henry Kissinger came in 1976 to lay out the Ford administration's policy for southern Africa as revolts against white minority rule in South Africa and what was then Rhodesia were intensifying.

Clinton, on the first leg of a three-nation tour of Africa, arrived in

Zambia from the United Arab Emirates, where she attended an international conference on Libya. After Zambia, she heads to Tanzania and Ethiopia before returning to Washington next week.

Written By MATTHEW LEE

What a powerful speech indeed. Nigerians should not trivialize the issue of financial enslavement by the Asians and other interested countries, because debtors (African countries) will forever remain at the mercy of their creditors (Asians and other countries). Re-colonization should not yet be the talk of the day, until the new Nigerian leaders refuse to embrace changes that would get the country to start moving towards greatness. If Nigerian leaders reject reforms that would curb excessive political waste, and move the country towards becoming the next engine of global growth, then Nigerians should be ready to welcome their new colonial masters likely China, India and America.

The race is now on for the conquest of Nigeria, once the incoming administration fails to salvage the country, and this is more reasons why Nigerians should massively support the Muhammadu Buhari government to succeed; failure cannot be an option, Nigeria must surely survive by fire by force, God willing. Withholding of massive support that would enable the new government to purge chronic corruption and move the country forward would definitely be a grievous mistake that Nigerians would forever live to regret, because the era of poor masses' intimidations and manipulations are being eliminated from the global village.

CHAPTER 6

The Way Forward

America is one of the greatest countries of the world today, because the nation's stakeholders boldly but reluctantly confronted the big issue of racial divide in the 1960s; South African government with global help, confronted the biggest challenge of apartheid in the 1970s to move the country forward. Today, the challenge of chronic corruption is threatening to destroy Nigerians; can the global village also encourage and motivate Nigerians to boldly confront the challenge and move African giant forward? When a nation fails to study and talk about the dreadful past mistakes in national building process like in Nigeria, the people will definitely forget, and the past mistakes would likely be repeated with much deadlier consequences. Contrary to most of the viewpoints that have been expressed towards the Nigerian civil war, intellectually gifted and very articulate individuals can construe that the civil war resulted from a failed attempt to kill chronic corruption in the country. The then Nigerian army was dominated by certain people from one tribal group, unfortunately, some of the visionary young officers who were not happy the way the politicians were dividing the country with their hate speeches and the ongoing massive looting of Nigerian treasury planned to put a stop to such unhealthy actions of the politicians.

One of the coup planners that were supposed to kill the political leader of the major ethnic group failed in his mission while others killed the other political leaders of the other two major ethnic groups. The killing failure was all the politicians needed to plunge the country into a deadly civil war, because the politicians connived with the military to start killing the innocent and harmless people from the tribe that dominated the army; accusing them of selective approach to eliminate all Nigerians. Nobody can say for sure what would have happened in the country, if a coalition of external powers led by president Barrack Obama of America had not insisted that the masses will prevail, the outcome of the March presidential election would have been business as usual and the hungry poor masses might set the country burning.

One of the biggest challenges facing the unity and upward movement of Nigeria today is genuine political reforms that would present strong opposition which would act as watch dog to the government in power. Needless to say that without a strong opposition party in the country, wrestling Nigeria away from chronic corruption might be an indefinable exercise to say the least. The new government should and must be encouraged by every Nigerian to make sure that the People Democratic Party (PDP), the party that lost the March 28th 2015 presidential election will join forces with other minor parties and form a strong opposition to the new government.

Nigeria has accepted and dwelt in chronic corruption for many decades, and curbing it now requires sacrifices from every Nigerian, her colonial master and the global village. Previous governments failed to curb chronic corruption in the past because Nigerians never accepted that there was anything like corruption in the country, and if the new administration would not garner enough support from the masses, the chances would be another failed government. Contrary to what everyone is saying that leadership is the major problem of Nigeria, the author has constantly maintained that Nigerian problem is the masses and not the leaders, because leaders are mirror images of a nation. Nigerians must therefore refuse chronic corruption first, before they lend their unconditional support to the new administration to kill deadly sources of chronic corruption.

Challenges from Robots and Advanced Technology

Robot is defined as a mechanical device configured with computer programs to perform a specific task. A robot can be independent or semi-independent depending on the builders' objectives. Robotics is a branch of technology that deals with design, construction, operation and the computer programs that runs robots. America and other developed countries are becoming increasing productive because of the alarming use of robots and other artificial intelligence software. In the early 19th century in America, over seventy percent (70%) rely on farm work for their livelihood, but today, the use of automation and other robots took most of the jobs and left less than two percent (2%) of the American work force in the farming industry. The displaced workers luckily found jobs created by the great wave of automation that enveloped mankind in recent years.

Automation really served mankind because it made countries that embraced automation more productive and gave the countries undue economic advantages over other nations that failed to embrace the wave of innovation. Why would the team of outgoing Nigerian president Goodluck Jonathan be bragging that they are diversifying the country's economy with a technologically conquered agricultural economic sector that cannot absorb up to 8% of Nigerian labor force?

Now that robots are being increasing used to replace many of the jobs created by automation, mankind is beginning to wonder what will be the next move to save the jobs of million people in the world. The increasing use of Artificial Intelligence (AI) in robots and other mechanical devices are very scary because the programs are turning those robots into semi-human beings, because robots can now think or pre-empt what humans can do next, based on documented and analyzed pattern of behaviors on human beings by the robots. Many might be wondering if this discussion is important in the book, actually it is more important than any other topic because Nigeria and other African leaders really need to start being proactive to future projections. Can you imagine what will happen to a nation that cannot create enough jobs for the growing youths getting enveloped with the automation wave to make the country productive?

Robots are increasingly consolidating their gains in already-automated industries in our global village making the cheap labor advantage Nigeria and other African countries had over Western countries obsolete. After robots finish replacing assembly line workers, they will replace the workers in warehouses. Robots that can lift up to 250 pounds all day long will now retrieve boxes, sort them, and load them onto trucks. Fruit and vegetable picking will continue to be robotized until no humans pick outside of specialty farms. Pharmacies will feature a single pill-dispensing robot in the back while the pharmacists focus on patient consulting. Next, the more dexterous chores of cleaning in offices and schools are being taken over by robots that can work 365 days without any sick leave and overtime pays. The robots are now starting with the easy-to-do floors and windows and will eventually get to all parts of the building. The highway legs of long-haul trucking routes will be driven by robots embedded in truck cabs. Modern cars might eventually be equipped with robots that can drive humans anywhere they want to go. Commercial bank tellers, monitoring guards, cleaners, drivers, etc., will soon be replaced by robots in the not too distant future.

This is actually the more reason Nigerians cannot afford to let chronic corruption remain in their country for another year, because the country is already behind in the race for productivity. Nigerians are very hard working people, but they need to purge themselves of chronic corruption and help their leaders to achieve excellence in their leadership roles. For how long can Nigerians take their exuberant and promising leaders and turn them into the most hated monsters when the leaders leave offices? This new administration cannot be allowed to fail because the consequences of their failure will be devastating to Nigeria and the entire continent, so please help, make your sacrifices and give the new (Muhammadu Buhari and Yemi Osinbajo)administration an unreserved support to organically and efficiently grow the economy.

On February 11, 2011, some hours after the Egyptian's revolution ended, President Barrack Obama said that history has just been made, because some people's voices had been heard in Africa. Today April 11th 2015, another history has just been made in Africa because the foreign policy of President Barrack Obama has witnessed the first time there was a smooth transition of power from one political power to another in Nigeria. It is now very important to have a handover of power from the old administration so that the masses can see the effect of changes brought about by the collective efforts of global village. If the handover process in May 29th of 2015 fails, the country might degenerate back into military regimes that will usher in bloody coups once again. This is a new era in Nigerian democratic institutions and all Nigerians must make genuine efforts and sacrifices in order to start moving the country in the right direction.

There are two real fundamental issues confronting Nigeria, and to the extent the issues are address and resolved will be a determinant factor for the future place of Nigeria in the global village. The two issues are constitutional and utilization of human resources. All hands must be on deck to urgently address these destructive issues, because the unintended consequences of not addressing those issues contributed immensely to the growth of chronic corruption in the country. The government must have a thorough review of her constitution and then reach out to Nigerian professionals in Diaspora and together they can accomplish the target goal of a dream Nigeria.

A constitution is the body of rules, which directly or indirectly affects the distribution, or the exercise of the sovereign power in the nation state. It is the collection of principles according to which the powers of any government and the right of the general public are adjustably based. It affects the distribution and exercise of the sovereignty of a state or union. It details how the wealth of a nation state should be managed and equally distributed among the nationals and also how unlawful offenders should be punished.

A. Constitutional Issues

Nigeria, as a matter of urgency, needs to revisit the constitutions left behind by her colonial master and military dictators; and make sure that these constitutions are in tandem with all the diverging ethnic groups that made up the country. If the lapses are so much, the inherited constitutions must be discarded and new ones need to be implemented; a new constitution that will be true reflections of the aspirations of the diverging groups put together. The new Constitutions will come from transparent dialogue between all the converging tribes; that will be from the people, by the people, and for the people, and not constitutions designed for the selfish interests of some groups of people or by past Nigerian dictators.

A constitution that will create checks and balances by sharing power equally to the three arms of Nigerian government; namely: executive, judiciary, and legislative. The new constitutional edifice will definitely take away the absolute powers given to Nigerian President and institute power checking mechanism that would prevent subsequent abuse of power. Leadership failures in the country are entrenched in the Nigerian constitution that empowers the president and governors to legally spend unaccounted billions of money on security related issues every month without explaining how the money was spent. Such illegal empowerment in the Constitution gave rise to monster presidents and governors who used their unimpeded rights to abuse the masses at will. If this behavior is not expunged from the Constitution which encourages these leaders to run the country as their personal companies, then eliminating chronic corruption in Nigeria might be another lip syncing exercise. Towns/Villages must also be constitutionally empowered to hold political elections that would produce the social, economic, financial and political leaders of such areas.

The new administration's first month in office will definitely set the stage for the fight on chronic corruption, because if the president can purge the presidential excess that have been enjoyed by the past leaders, the whole nation must solidly stand behind him in the epic battle to win war against chronic corruption in the country. How can the Nigerian president and legislative chamber members earn more than the developed countries that are more productive? The masses must definitely encourage the most loved president of Nigeria Muhammadu Buhari (based on his past performance) to start the war on chronic corruption from the violated presidential office.

Nigerians must collectively win the battle of chronic corruption which will enable them to see the other vices that are destroying their country. The economic effects of continue job loss from automation and robots must start getting prioritize in the scale of economic challenges facing the country. Once again, let Nigerians start making their leaders more productive and proactive instead of laid back leaders the masses have produced in the past years. Nigerians are constantly talking about how evil and corrupt their leaders are, because they really have not helped the leaders to be more upright by simply purging chronic corruption in their lives. They are the ones that produced those leaders, and leaders are mirror images of their followers. Bad and chronically corrupt masses must definitely produce chronically corrupt leaders because an eagle can never give birth to a vulture.

B. Use of human resources (Nigerians in Diaspora)

There might be a great danger ahead for Nigerians in the event that Nigerian stakeholders refuse to reach out to Nigerian professionals in Diaspora, because these are group of Nigerians that can take bold lead in creating small and medium scale industries in the country. Nigerian leaders must get Nigerian professionals in Diaspora deeply involved in any transparent attempt in building a new Nigeria that will compete effectively in the global village. Nigerian professionals in Diaspora are more or less outsiders and the country needs many of them to come and showcase what knowledge they have acquired from many years of sojourning outside their motherland. Make no mistake; if these groups of Nigerians are motivationally encouraged to come back home and help in nation building, the country will definitely be a better place within 10 years.

However, Nigerian leaders have limited time to harness the potential of Nigerian professionals in Diaspora, because the bulk of these Nigerian professionals are from the baby boomer generation; and they have begun their retirement in 2011. A good investment estimate on the government of Nigeria is that any $1 spent in bringing back Nigerian professionals in Diaspora will directly or indirectly return $10 to both the federal and state governments. Let the federal and state governments jointly go after these groups of Nigerians because their returns will definitely pay off in short time.

Nigerian professionals in Diaspora will be the ones to dove-tail other expatriates and professionals that will come to Nigerian and make the country financially and economically relevant in the world economy, because the professionals have already established good lines of credit while in Diaspora. Nigerian professionals in Diaspora are one of the greatest resources that Nigerian leaders must have to find ways of utilizing, because they might be holding up the four aces that would help to tower the country to a globally respected height. Getting back Nigerian professionals in Diaspora to Nigeria might be a very difficult task to accomplish; but the following might help speed up the process:

1. Creation of ministries with fewer bureaucracies

2. Federal and State governments' incentive packages

3. Security protections

1. Creation of ministries with fewer bureaucracies

The Nigerian government needs to start creating ministries that would cater to the needs of returning Nigerian professionals in Diaspora, and these ministries must be headed by one of the returned Nigerian professionals in Diaspora from such an area. Each ministry must be departmentalized into the following areas:

• European Nigerian professionals

• Asian Nigerian professionals

• Australian Nigerian professionals

• American Nigerian professionals

• Middle Eastern Nigerian professionals

• Other Nigerian professionals

A professional that came back from a particular area of the world must head that department, because that person is very conversant with that area and probably understands the technicalities of the needs of such Nigerians out there. The departmental heads will embark on headhunts in those particular areas they returned from, because they relate very well with those Nigerians in that part of the globe. The department heads need not go to these areas empty-handed, because the professionals would want to know what is in there for them, based on the risk they would take; they must go to these places with the federal and state governments' enticement packages. Successful creation of these ministries will depend on how much the Nigerian leaders were able to eliminate favoritism and nepotism from the appointment of those administrators. Five million gainful employments can be created yearly in Nigerian, if this project can annually bring back just ten percent (10%) of Nigerian professionals in Diaspora.

Assumptions

The author is using a conservative number of about ten million Nigerians in Diaspora, and the following percentages are:

- 10,000,000 number of Nigerian professionals in Diaspora

- 1,000,000 being 10% of Nigerian professionals in Diaspora

- 5 jobs per those lured back Nigerian professionals in Diaspora

All assumptions are based on the projections that the 10% of Nigerian professionals in Diaspora would be lured back home with some incentives from all the national, and state governments; these professionals can comfortably create 5,000,000 jobs annually. This is just an average of five career jobs generated by each one of those lured back Nigerians; examples of such jobs

- Drivers

- Cooks

- Gardeners

- Maids

- Gatemen/Guards

Let us also be mindful that some of these returning Nigerians in Diaspora might be coming home with the mindset of setting up factories; thereby creating more middle class employment for Nigerians. Let the policy makers consider these groups of Nigerians seriously because there is a hidden treasure in getting some of them back home, instead of having them send billions every year to their loved ones.

2. Federal and State governments' incentive packages

Federal and State governments would have to strategize with commercial banks on how to encourage the Nigerian professionals in Diaspora to come and establish new industries in the country. Some key positions in these new industries would specifically be reserved for Nigerian professionals in Diaspora that would help them to give these industries western flavor and style of management and at the same time creating the much needed export trades to their sojourned countries. Some key positions in these industries will have some very attractive pay packages that will target Nigerian professionals in Diaspora, because most of them would not want to engage in fraudulent activities. Nigeria government using Nigerian professionals in Diaspora to lead in the country's industrial revolution would definitely help the country by increasing their export trades and at the same time increase capital inflows into the country.

State governments must also set aside certain percentage of their annual budgets which will serve as matching funds for any Nigerian professional in Diaspora that are coming back to Nigeria to set up vetted and proven project in any of the states. Some of the returning professionals in Diaspora should be able to receive certain funds at very low interest rates to help implode the number of industries in the country. Like earlier mentioned that any $1 spent by the governments on Nigerians in Diaspora to come home and create some jobs, should bring back to the governments a return of over $10 in the no distant time, because the jobs that would be created by those groups of Nigerians would help generate monthly disposable incomes into many households, and the households will turn around and spend the money into the economy.

Three to five years tax incentives should also be given to any company or industry set up by any Nigerian professional in Diaspora. State lands need to be made available to Nigerian professionals in Diaspora that are setting up industries in an industrial designated area only. Commercial banks should receive low interest rate funds from the federal and state government in their budget for industrialization of their respective states using a combination of Nigerians in Diaspora and other graduates in the country.

3. Security Protections

One of the biggest concerns of Nigerians in Diaspora returning to Nigeria is the yearly growing insecurity of lives and properties in the country. Stories of Nigerians in Diaspora who lost their lives to men of the under-ground world in Nigeria are on the rise. The worst of it all is that the majority of the perpetuators of such horrendous murders and kidnappings were never caught to face the law, and because of that, more unemployed youths are joining the underground economic activities. A random opinion poll of two hundred Nigerians in Diaspora in the course of writing this book revealed some shocking information.

Amazingly, ninety percent (90%) of those polled indicated security as their biggest concern in going to Nigeria. The recent increase of Nigerians in Diaspora visiting home is even escalating an already charged atmosphere of suspended fear. Hello Nigerian government! Any short-term remedy to address this insecurity issue, while modalities are being worked out for an everlasting long-term solution?

It is the exclusive responsibility of all Nigerian nationals to promote, protect, and preserve the values of the land, but when the governments at all levels fail to perform their own part of protection, the poor masses are left at the mercies of the Nigerian surging armed and criminal gangsters. All Nigerians must graciously and collectively join their forces together to combat chronic corruption and address the security issues in Nigeria so that investment opportunities will open up by creating more meaningful developments and economic booms in the country. It is quite possible that Nigeria can be made into the new frontier for global village economic boom, once Nigerians encourage and support their leaders to eliminate chronic corruption in the country. Eliminating chronic corruption in the country definitely would not be an easy task, but the masses lining behind their new leaders can get it done.

A well-articulated move to attract Nigerian professionals in Diaspora will have to start by addressing their issues of security concerns. If the governments cannot convincingly address the issues of security concerns of Nigerian professionals in Diaspora, the governments should not even consider including them in the Nigerian rebirth game plan; as any effort to bring them back will be an exercise in futility. Remember that some of these Nigerian graduates in Diaspora with rusticated certificates will be quick to jump at any offer to return home, while those with active certificates might be reluctant to give up their good existing jobs. The treasure is hidden in Nigerian professionals in Diaspora who are still working in their fields of disciplines. Any Nigerian professional in Diaspora that has not worked with his certificate for over 10 years really does not have much to offer to the country.

A good starting point in addressing the security lapses in Nigeria will have to start with the federal government including towns/villages in the power and revenue sharing formulas of the country, and also encourage states, local government areas, and towns to set up their own police services for accountability. The existing federal policing laws in the country must definitely be reviewed and repackaged for more effective and efficient security in the country, here are some review suggestions:

- Over centralization of the Police Force

- Police paid poor packages

- Lack of modern training & equipment

- Re-integrating the police officers with the public.

Over Centralization of the police force

All over the world, it has been proven that over centralization kills establishments. This is the primary reason big corporate bodies and other public establishments are being broken down (decentralized) into manageable numbers. Some corporate bodies will even spin off divisions as full-fledged independent companies. Why should the Nigerian Government continue to dwell in the past by over centralizing the police force hoping to adequately protect the lives and properties of the masses?

Take for instance in Nigeria today, all decisions have to come from one police boss., This makes it easier to use the police force to rig elections and commit other atrocities in Nigeria, because you have only one person to lobby. The incoming administration really has to deeply look into decentralizing the police force if they hope to achieve their pride slogan of protecting lives and properties of all Nigerians. Can anybody imagine what would happen in Nigeria today if the police system is decentralized all the way to villages for adequate accountability? With autonomous powers to protect Nigerians in their jurisdictions the country would definitely be on the path of greatness.

The independent police systems would now be held accountable for major criminal activities that happen in their areas of responsibility. You can rest be assured that security in the country would automatically improve overnight.

A decentralized police force all the way to the numerous villages giving the police autonomous powers would undoubtedly bring efficiency and accountability to the Nigerian Police Force once again. In the 1970s and early 1980s Nigerians slept in front of their houses, without fear of anything, because chronic corruption had not yet advanced to the current stage. . Today, however, before you can attempt such things, you better make sure that you have a current will in place. Your family might think something is wrong with you. They might wonder why you want to commit suicide.

In today's Nigeria people have to spend large amounts of money to burglar proof their houses to deter armed robbers. Yet in some areas, the armed robbers still come in and have a field day without any interference from the law. A decentralized Nigerian Police Force would bring in competition, accountability, and checks and balances among the decentralized units. The Nigerian Police could be decentralized in the following format:

- Federal Police Services

- The State Police Services

- The Local Government Area Police Services

- Town Police Services

Federal Police Services The Federal Government of Nigeria should have and maintain their own police bureaus in all corners of the country. Then they can be called upon to handle all crimes classified as federal crimes. In addition to being visible in all parts of the country, the bureaus will also have the jurisdiction to investigate state, local governments, and town police bureaus to make sure that they do not engage in nepotism and tribalism policing. This would be another step in checking chronic corruption and electoral malpractice in the country.

The federal police should also act as a watchdog in the event of unfair and unjust arrests of minorities (people who were unjustly treated because they are from other states). The size of the Federal Police Force should be relative to the population of the nation. Any federal police agent should have a minimum of one year attending classes from reputable colleges. The federal police bureau should have branches in all the states even village levels. The federal courts must be ready for quick trials, dispensing cases that come into the federal courts.

The State Police forces The state police should be completely independent from the federal police bureaus. They should be allowed to formulate strategies that will help them maintain law and order in their particular state. It should also be the duty and responsibility of the state police force to make sure that lives and properties are safeguarded in their state. State police forces will be accountable for all crimes committed in their respective states. The federal police will take over cases classified as federal crimes and dispense those cases within a short period of time, because justice delayed is actually justice denied.
Nigerians should be encouraged to settle their cases in the court of law, but due to unnecessary delays in courts, sometimes over 5 years; Nigerians use physical forces and sometimes hire assassins to settle their case. Please create jobs for Nigerian Lawyers by making sure that cases are tried and dismissed within a one year period, because that would help to increase the number of people patronizing Lawyers..

They should also have branches in local government areas of those particular states which act as watchdogs over the federal and local government police services. The size and population of the state will determine the number of police officers needed for effective and efficient policing of each state..

States should also have their own courts that will give quick trials to cases that come to the courts. They can also sue and be sued by any individual that feels aggrieved or denied justice.

The Local Government Area Police Services The local

government police forces should be responsible and accountable for lives and properties in those particular local government areas. They should also be completely independent from the state's police force. Formulation and implementation of strategies that will help maintain law and order in the local government areas will lie squarely on their shoulders. The size and population of the local government will determine the number and size of the police force needed to safeguard the local government areas.

The ratio should not be more than one police officer per one hundred people. Local government areas must also set up courts to quickly try incidents that occur in their respective local government areas within one year of the offence so that other citizens who feel aggrieved will not take the law into their own hands.

Town Police Services The town police services will also be completely independent from the local government police services. They would be the primary custodians of the lives and properties in their towns.

Since the town police services have larger constituencies, they should be motivationally configured to generate the bulk of their revenue from traffic and criminal offenders in those towns. The town police officers should be given good pay and benefit packages to deter them from accepting bribes from the public.

The population and size of the town would also be used to determine the number of police officers that will take care of the town. There is no doubt whatsoever that the decentralization of the police force in Nigeria will create competition and efficient policing in the entire country.

Towns should also set up their own courts for quick trials of suspected law offenders. The federal, state and local police should watch town police to make sure that tribal, discriminatory, and bigotry policing is not taking place in town.

Some people might argue that because of ethnic diversity of Nigerians, state, local governments, town police will use the opportunity to victimize the non-indigenous people in those areas. Well, some scholars really do not think that such an argument will hold water, because such victimization of non-indigenous people will be a federal crime, and any officer found guilty will be convicted, and punished accordingly.

The town police will not have an incentive to victimize non-indigenous people of such a town when they know very well that the victim will take the case to the local government police and if necessary, all the way to federal police. The major advantage of decentralizing the Nigerian police force will be the creation of competition among federal, state, and local governments and town police in solving crimes. This will bring in checks and balances in Nigeria. Competition always brings out the best from any organization, while protection and over centralization will kill organizations. Let Nigerian policy makers get down to work and save the country from decades of ignorant leadership that is threatening to turn the masses against their leaders.

To create checks and balances, any person that feels that the Town court denied him/her justice can appeal his/her case from the Local government court to State, and Federal court, all the way to the Supreme Court. Do you know that millions of jobs could also be created to accommodate the new lawyers that would be graduating from Law colleges every year. At the same time, millions of Nigerians would now be encouraged to go to court and seek redress instead of resorting to juggle justice?

Poor Police Pay Packages

It is amazing that the Nigerian police officers are among the least paid workers in the country. How do Nigerians expect efficient protection from professional officers that are not well motivated? Men and women who put their lives on the line to protect the public are the worst paid. Something is terribly wrong with this system?

Well, as a result of the police poor pay packages, the Nigerian police have justifiably succeeded in institutionalizing bribery and corruption in the country. Who can blame the police officers for setting up check points (actually toll booths) where they religiously extort monies from the public to make up for the short fall in their peanut salaries? Let the policy makers decentralize the Nigerian police force and pay the young officers very well and weed out the bad police officers among them. Nigerian Police Officers will be made to account for their new pay structure. That would help to deter them from accepting bribes from the masses.

The poor pay package is actually the primary reason corruption is growing faster than both Nigerian GDP and population combined. The majority of Nigerian police officer's pay package is less than $3,000.00 per annum. Chronic corruption breeds bribery, and bribery breeds destruction. This is why no police officer should be paid anything less than fifteen thousand American Dollars equivalent to $15,000.00 per annum. Such a pay system as well as other reward incentive packages would make it impossible for these fine officers to accept bribes There should be a minimum of ten (10) years imprisonment for any police officer caught accepting a bribe.

Do you really expect Nigerian Police Officers to arrest somebody he just took a bribe from? Any field police officer should be made to earn his salary. At least, an officer should be expected to arrest a certain number of criminals, traffic offenders and law breakers in any given quarter. If he meets his target, he will be rewarded, and if he misses the target, he should be punished or even fired from the police service.

Let the Nigerian Government pay these fine police officers very well, decentralize and reposition the officers for efficient and effective policing in Nigeria. Let the Nigerian Police Officers be in the forefront of fighting chronic corruption in the country, since Nigerians have come to see the average police officer as the epitome of chronic corruption.

There should also be enough insurance coverage on the lives of these fine officers that are willing to sacrifice their lives for the masses. Life insurance coverage of at least, $50,000 is needed to insure their economic value to their loved ones and motivate the wonderful police officers to do their work prudentially. Such actions would help make police officers more efficient and productive.

More time is being spent on the issue of security since it is the oxygen through which the nation breathes. Once Nigeria has an efficient security system in place, millions of jobs will be created that would absorb some of those who are still waiting in the unemployment labor market. Restaurants, department stores, filling stations and some other companies can now operate on a double or even a triple-shift basis, thereby creating more jobs. Solve security problem in Nigeria by decentralizing the police force and automatically generate additional two million jobs, and reduce the crime rate by at least 20%.

Let's not encourage the Nigerians that sell cell phones and recharge cards in the day and in the night engage in the underground economy as contributing to Nigerian GDP, because their criminal side effects are more than they are contributing to the national gross domestic products.

Lack of modern training and up-to-date equipment

After decentralization of Nigerian Police Force, police officers should be adequately trained and equipped for effective and efficient policing. Police Officers' current level of training and equipment will not be a match for the modern and more sophisticated equipment being used by the men of the underworld in some parts of Nigeria.

In addition to the modern training, police officers should have a certain number of college credit hours, preferably in human psychology. The college courses will help them to interrelate and communicate more effectively with the public; thereby limiting police brutality.

Police officers should be equipped with brand new cars for official use only. Any officer caught using the car for a personal use should be fired. All police officers, both off and on-duty, must carry guns at all times, and no car that is more than three (3) years old should be found in the police's fleet of cars. All field police officers must be physically and mentally fit at all times, and any police officer that is not fit should be fired or get into the back office.

Re-integration of police officers with the public

The Nigerian Police Officers by commission or omission have been segregated from the public and quartered in police barracks. This doesn't give the police officers enough time to access and profile the citizens in their areas of policing. The police officers need to constantly interact with the public on 24-hour basis to be able to understand what any individual is capable of doing at any given point in time. The idea of segregating police officers from the public must be stopped immediately because the police officers really need to have endless interaction with their surroundings.

Police officers need to constantly study and monitor the behavior of the public. The constant monitoring and study of public behaviors will help the police officers pre-empt criminal minds before such minds go to work. Community policing has resulted in positive efficient and effective protection of lives and properties in many countries, such as the United States of America and other developed nations. Does anyone say that Nigeria cannot emulate such noble programs once the nation has subdued chronic corruption?

Re-integrating the police officers with the public will help the officers in profiling the likely criminal offenders and even dissuade would be criminal offender in such areas to either move out of such areas or stop their criminal activities. Police officers should be encouraged to work in areas where they are residing. This will give them advantage in trying to maintain law and order in that neighborhood because the officers would get to know more of the people in their neighborhood. An average Nigerian really would not mind having quality trained police officers as neighbors because the police officers might intervene in any attack or crime in the neighborhood.

Think about it for a minute. You are getting twenty-four police protection by virtue of your accommodation, as a matter of fact Nigerians would not mind paying 20% more taxes for such services, provided such officers live up to expectations of their neighbors when being attacked. What do you think will happen if men of the under-ground world are attacking such neighborhoods? Well, if the police officer who lives in the neighborhood did not show up or call for immediate re-enforcement, then it will be obvious that such an officer has to answer for his inaction.

Nigerian Police Officers' constant interactions with the public will help them to anticipate and pre-empt crimes before they are even committed. The police officers must be re-integrated with the public for effective and efficient protection of lives and properties of the entire public because many Nigerians are seeing the police officers as the epitome of criminal activities.

The Nigerian government really needs to decentralize, and change the image of the Nigerian Police Force, so that the masses would start having confidence in them again. The chronic corruption in the country has gone beyond all the corners of the country making the police officers, who are the chief law enforcement officers lead the attack that would eliminate the deadly vices of chronic corruption in the country, would definitely be a welcome development in Nigeria.

CHAPTER 7

Education

Muhammadu Buhari, the newly elected president of the most populous black nation in the world must urgently break up the Nigerian police force, decentralize and reprogram them if he really wants to win the battle of chronic corruption, because decentralization of the police departments would also act as a watchdog. Like mentioned earlier in the book if any Nigerian can win over the deadly evil of chronic corruption, Buhari is the most qualified person for such a job. He has the anointed man of God (Vice President Yemi Osinbajo) with him so all he needs right now is to get support of 70% of the country's poor masses to do the work.

According to Wikipedia, Education in its general sense is a form of learning in which the knowledge, skills and habits of a group of people are transferred from one generation to the next through teaching, training, and research. Education frequently takes place under the guidance of others, but may also be autodidactic.

 Any experience that has a formative effect on the way one thinks, feels, or acts may be considered educational. On the other hand, Education could be defined as the process of transferring knowledge, skills and values from one or group of individuals to others. Without the basic necessary education, man is nothing more than animals. Actually, the less educated individuals are more vulnerable for recruitment by radical and militancy groups, because the truths are hidden in the books that they lack the knowledge to read and assimilate the contents. Education that was transferred from one generation to the other has placed man above other living creatures, and will continue to advance technology for the use of mankind.

The acquired knowledge from Education helps man to think ecologically, understand the interconnectedness of humans and natural systems. At the same time it develops capacity to apply this understanding so that human communities and natural ecosystems may co-exist peacefully. The capacity to transfer knowledge to many Nigerians and other African countries is being hampered by the following: religious beliefs, cost of education, limited educational facilities and poor pay packages for teachers.

Religious beliefs; Certain religions forbid their followers from pursuing advanced levels of education while others prohibit any form of knowledge acquisition in the country. A deeper probe into some of these religious beliefs might reveal that the custodians of such religious groups might be trying to change the laws by themselves as such prohibition is against the fundamentals of those religions. This actually could have been a handiwork of chronic corruption as the political leaders are desperately trying to hide the truth from the poor masses.

Cost of education: cost of virtually everything in Nigeria and other African countries has been rising beyond the reach of over 75% of Africans; so many Africans no longer see the required investments to acquire knowledge as a worthy one. Nigerian Government failed to build and train enough teachers to handle the huge population surge from the seventies, and the scarcity of schools and teachers made the cost of education for poor masses very exorbitant. Many Nigerians from the southern part of the country are willing to engage themselves in two or more jobs just to train their kids in schools, but the jobs are not available.

Limited educational facilities: Chronic corruption really took a big chunk of the money that was set aside for the growth of education in Nigeria and the resources being allocated to education has increasingly been on the downside ever since the colonial master left the shores of the country. It might be really difficult to go through the fiscal budgets of Nigeria and other African countries and see up to 25% being allocated to educational related needs.

Teachers' Poor pay packages: Nigerian teachers are the ones that bear the crucial burden of chronic corruption because every administration's spending cuts normally starts with education, while the political class fat salaries are always intact. Since the Teachers are being poorly paid in the country, they have resorted to other means of making ends meet, thereby reducing the quality of knowledge being passed down from one generation to another. The future of any group of people is greatly tied the level and quality of knowledge being passed from one generation to another, and if Nigeria has failed in making adequate provision for transfer of knowledge, then the future of the country will definitely be questionable.

Can Nigeria become a global engine of growth without adequate educational systems to transfer knowledge, skills and values from one generation to another? Nigerian leaders must start spending nothing less than 30% of Nigeria's annual budget on education, if only the excessive government waste can accommodate such educational provisions. Yes! The country is still thousands of miles away from being the next engine of global growth, without adequate growth in educational system, because the country's past dictators destroyed the learning institutions to make sure that the students would not join forces and rise up against their regimes.

Chronic corruption has destroyed the country's educational system because the learning institutions were compromised to make sure that keeping the masses in perpetual bondage will continue. The new administration must place education as one of its top priorities because the future of the country depends on the quality of students that pass from the higher institutions. The deadly students' cultism in the country's learning institutions today is the handiwork of a corrupt political class that used those kids as tugs in achieving an ill political objective in the country. Pleasing the masses should help President Buhari to restructure and restore the dignity of Nigerian students because the future of all Nigerians lies on the students' shoulders.

Role of government in Education

The right to acquire education has been created and recognized by some jurisdictions. Since 1952 Article 2 of the first Protocol to the European Convention on Human Rights obliges all signatory parties to guarantee the right to education. It does not however guarantee any particular level of education or any particular quality. At the global level, the United Nations' International Covenant on Economic, Social and Cultural Rights of 1966 guarantees this right under Article 13. The three forms of learning as defined by Organization for Economic Cooperation and Development (OECD) are Formal, Informal and Non-formal Education.

Systems of schooling that involve institutionalized teaching and learning in relation to a curriculum, which itself is established according to a predetermined purpose of the schools in the system, are very vital in building any nation. Kindergarten, preschool, primary and, secondary and higher learning institutions are all forms of learning systems that are very crucial in preparing man how to co-exist with fellow man in our global village. The image of Nigerian Professional Teachers have been so degraded that a majority of Nigerians do not want to have anything to do with teachers. The teachers have been deprived of timely pay of their peanut salaries, because the government felt that their services are not really important in the country. But a house of representative member makes about the salary of more than 100 teachers put together.

The teachers were indirectly configured to pass a half-baked quality of knowledge to the kids because they have to engage in other petty trades to make ends meet since their salaries are not forthcoming on a monthly basis. Little or no research is being carried out in the nation's universities because chronic corruption takes away the money allocated to research. What kind of a future awaits a nation that destroys the educational system?

When the military dictators were destroying the country's educational system, little did they think about the unintended consequences of their actions? Today, it will take a big fight and collective efforts of all Nigerians to restore the many decades of our destroyed educational system.

Take a very good look at the quality of students passing out of Nigerian higher learning institutions today. No wonder parents that can afford it send their children abroad to go study. If you are satisfied with the quality then you need to know that Nigeria can have a better future. If you are not satisfied with things as they are then quickly join forces with the new president to eradicate chronic corruption in the country.

The greatness of any nation depends on the nation's ability to invest handsomely in the nation's educational system. That would produce quality leaders in the future. Knowledge is an asset. Information is power that will always place any nation above her equals. Knowledge must be vigorously pursued by any nation that wants to remain relevant in the global village. The only thing that great countries of our global village have in common is the huge amount of money they invest in their educational systems. Nigerian military leaders undoubtedly started the chronic and malicious destruction of all spheres of education in the country, and today the nation is witnessing the result of the destructions through the surging criminal families that partake in kidnapping, stealing and raping the young girls and engaging in political turmoil.

Nigerian Military Leaders in the past years have destroyed most of the learning institutions that the colonial master was able to put in place. As the quality of education continues to drastically go down in the country, the cost of education has become out of the reach of over 75% of Nigerians, making education an undesirable luxury in the country. The time to start rebuilding the educational systems in Nigeria is now! But can the governments afford to pay for such services because more money is being spent on running the big Nigerian government?

Rebuilding Nigerian educational system would be the giant step towards making the country the next engine of global growth in the world. Quality education is one of the vital ingredients in building a strong and formidable nation because "knowledge is power and sharing that knowledge is empowerment". When a nation lacks quality educators, then the product of the nation's future leaders is in deep trouble, because the students that pass through the learning institutions will definitely have limited knowledge to help bring positive impacts in the country.

It might not be an overstatement to say that the majority of Nigerian graduates are less equipped with the necessary knowledge required to navigate the country away from the present direction of "bridge to nowhere". The future leaders of Nigeria are really in limbo, because the systematic failure in the country has actually marginalized and limited the scope of their intellectual prowess.

All hands must now be on deck to rebuild the Nigerian Educational System, if the country truly desires to be the next engine of growth because knowledge is power. The new administration is capable of quickly turning things around in the country, but would the masses give it their unconditional support to accomplish the task?

The time to rebuild the Nigerian educational system is now, because such a move will help to groom the future leaders into quality leaders of tomorrow. Nigerians can no longer afford to neglect their educational institutions because those young kids in schools are the mirror images of the tomorrow leaders.

Nigerian colonial master knew the importance of education. That was why large amounts of money was spent to build the Nigerian educational system from scratch. Nonetheless, when chronic corruption took over the policy makers in the country, educational funds were among the first funds that were embezzled, leaving the educational system with little or no money to even maintain the existing structures.

Unless the new administration will be willing to spend enough resources to start restoring and rebuilding the country's educational system, the future leaders of Nigeria might remain in a cloud of unknown destinations because garbage in, is equal to garbage out. Many countries are no longer recognizing degrees and diploma certificates from Nigeria because the quality of knowledge transfer in the country has been compromised.

CHAPTER 8

Future of Crude Oil and Nigeria

The discovery of coal caused the destruction of the demand for firewood as source of energy. Then crude oil came and knocked out coal. Today mankind is shopping for alternative sources of energy to help prevent our environment from heavy pollutants like coal and crude oil. Global warming is real and concerns are seriously building up on how to preserve our environment from untimely destruction, but how can environmental preservation be preached to Nigeria and many other African countries that are striving to survive?

As the global village has become overly concerned with the global warming conundrum, it is becoming obvious that all hands are getting on deck to help find a good solution to the nightmare to our dilapidating ozone layer. The Nigerian government needs to appoint individual officers that are proactively oriented so that they will articulate and pre-empt problems before they appear in the system. Nigerian leaders can no longer afford to be re-active oriented because the damages are so big and time-consuming to overcome.

There are two bench mark prices that are used by the global village to quote crude oil prices per barrel, Brent and WTI, but the most commonly used is Brent which is currently at $65 as of May 11th 2015. WTI crude oil which is of better quality than Brent was supposed to be more expensive, but as of May 11th 2015 when this book was being put together it was $59 per barrel, down from the October 2013 contract price for Brent crude oil that stood at $110.60 per barrel,. compared to the WTI current price of $50, against the $108.07 per barrel of October 2013.

This divergence in the price is actually telling us that something more sinister could definitely happen in the price of both WTI and Brent crude oils in the near future. Possibly very huge rises or sell-offs in both WTI and Brent crude oil prices could occur, but the author is of the opinion that Crude oil is more likely to get to $25 per barrel before heading back to $90 per barrel again.

The scenario of $125 or $25 barrel oil is highly possible in the near future, because certain policies, geo-political events, discoveries and tragedies can trigger such price variations in our global village. American auto manufacturing company Ford recently announced that they will soon be testing solar powered cars. Teasler; also a high technology auto manufacturing company has battery powered cars that can give individual owners up to 79 miles per gallon. Teasler recently announced that it would be going after residential and commercial electricity consumers; such action would further increase the demand destruction of crude oil. Technological breakthroughs are really attacking the demand for crude oil thereby creating a surplus of crude oil supplies than mankind would be able to absorb in any given year. Maybe the world is not paying enough attention to a recent test-flying of a solar powered air plane in March 2015. How soon can there be such solar powered airplanes available to the public?

It is also beginning to look as if mankind is much closer to the daily use of efficient alternative source of energy than we previously thought. Are governments now beginning to see the truth in climate changes and global warming threats to our precious environment?

Typically, WTI crude from Cushing Oklahoma America should bring a higher price than Brent Crude because it is a better quality, but the reverse is the case. The global effort to save our climate from manmade problems will negatively impact the prices of crude oil, whereby Nigeria and other African crude oil producing countries will definitely be the ultimate losers when that happens. It is urgent that Nigerian stakeholders and economists get on the drawing table with a sole mandate of diversifying the Nigerian economy away from a crude oil revenue based economy. It is urgent that Nigerian legislators pass a law that would free up some assets for the real economic diversification of the country's economy.

It is really unfortunate that many African policy makers have forgotten why crude oil prices got to over $100 per barrel in the first place, not realizing the same factors which quickly took the prices so high, will quickly bring down the prices once addressed? The global cost of borrowing is still low because the American Federal Reserve Board has not started increasing fed fund rate that would push the interest rates up. The Fed might still be on hold until the European Union finishes their own version of quantitative easing.

Summary of high crude oil prices: American economy ran into a big turbulence in 2007 that threatened to adversely affect the relevance of America in the global village. The policy makers had no choice but to devalue King Dollar, which made American goods and services very cheap and attractive to the global village. Consequently, crude oil and other commodity prices started skyrocketing to adjust for the devalued King Dollar because they were all quoted in dollars.

The King Dollar is quickly appreciating against other major currencies of the global village while American Federal Reverse has not yet started to tighten interest rates from the almost zero position it has been for a while. Expect crude oil prices to slide even further once the Fed walks away from zero interest rate policy. Sooner or later, it will happen because inflation is rearing its ugly head towards American economy.

Can one imagine what would happen to Nigeria and other crude oil producing nations when the American Federal Reserve starts raising interest rates in the future? Crude oil and other commodity prices will definitely start going down as King Dollar surges up. As a matter of fact, the King Dollar rising would definitely have adverse effects on the cost of capital in Africa because bank lending rates to the public will also jump from the current low 20% to maybe 30%. Such move would grind to a halt some economic activities in Nigeria and other countries.

The failure of Nigerian policy makers to adequately invest the excess crude oil funds from the previous years when crude oil prices have doubled in price will now hurt the economy.

Corruption and lack of future planning really took a big chunk of the excess crude reserve, and until Nigeria admits that corruption is a big problem, Nigerians might not unite to fight this anomaly. Expect the International Monetary Fund (IMF) and the World Bank to come knocking on the Nigerian government's door very soon, because the country's borrowing power has disappeared.

For months the deficit spending in Nigeria has been going up because, the falling crude oil prices have caused the country to supplement their monthly spending with her foreign reserve which is quickly going down. A large sum of the country's foreign and excess crude oil reserves were spent on the just concluded general elections while some was used to help save the currency from further slides against other major currencies.

No one can be absolutely sure about what will happen next in crude oil prices. Nevertheless, if pressured to make an educated guess, the author will say that the prices will most likely sell-off because of anticipated reductions in crude oil demand, rise in key interest rate in America, billions of American dollars being spent on the research of alternative energies, and the government's intensified efforts to create awareness of conservation of the environment

Crude oil price will most likely reach $25 per barrel before ever going back to $90 again, This is the primary reason Nigerian policy makers must rely on the input of investment advisors in Diaspora to help figure out how to harness all the hidden and nonperforming assets in the country.

Environmental consciousness is beginning to gain momentum in different quarters despite the fact that a predominant number of global village inhabitants are living below the United Nations defined poverty level of $2 per day.

Preservation of our environment is really getting to be the top priority of mankind's nightmare because certain unexplainable weather events are gradually but constantly taking places in our environment. Nigerian policy makers should be very careful when selecting and projecting their future source of energy, as wrong choices will definitely have adverse effects on their future GDP growth.

Since refining crude oil is one of major pollutants in our environment, gradual but intensifying pressures are mounting globally on politicians to look into and reduce mankind's over dependence on crude oil with a source of clean energy available.

We cannot imagine mankind doing away entirely with crude oil because we are in a world of crude oil. Nonetheless the unintended consequences of global policy makers not doing anything might be very grave. Crude oil now flows in our blood because virtually everything about our daily needs is directly or indirectly tied to crude oil.

Mankind's willingness to spill blood in order to satisfy this deadly, overzealous addiction will not stop, but continues to flow uninterrupted. Let Nigeria really look into alternative sources of energy, particularly environmentally friendly natural gas, and solar energy because they most likely will be the energy of the future.

It is quite unfortunate that uninterrupted access to crude oil can never and will never be compromised by the superpowers again, because in the past mankind paid higher prices when that happened. Remember our former addiction to coal which was reduced with the increased use of crude oil? Why would our political leaders keep denying the fact that solar energy and natural gas are capable of relegating crude oil as the first choice of future energy?

Can natural gas and other alternative sources of clean energy kill or reduce our overzealous addiction to crude oil? The author opines that the answer should be absolutely "Yes". It has happened in the past to firewood and coal, and chances are very high that crude oil will be replaced sooner than later.

Time will best answer these questions and vindicate the author's view point on the future of crude oil demand. because there are some underlying destructions that have not yet been manifested in our global village that would escalate the destruction. Nigerian policy makers once again are urgently advised to speed up their efforts to diversify their economy or jeopardize the economic and financial future of over 170,000,000 Nigerians.

President Muhammadu Buhari should surround himself with proactive thinking individuals who would help him achieve his age long goal of purging the country of chronic corruption.

Meanwhile, the Chinese economic policies that are slowing her economic growth plus austerity measures that are now playing out in European nations might be another catalyst to lower crude oil prices.

If crude oil prices go down sharply and by a large amount, then many African countries will have no choice other than to embrace austerity measures This action would further escalate the demand destruction and push crude oil price further down to $25 a barrel. Remember that selling begets selling on Wall Street.

Let the Nigerian government start looking for alternative source of revenue. One of them might be the land use act, which would make the government pass enabling laws that would include the villages and towns in power and a revenue sharing formula. Nigerian Villages are saturated with billions of dollars' worth of houses that do not have economic values. The owners cannot borrow or sell the houses to other persons again, because village houses are entirely different from city houses.

Monetization of these socially induced village nonperforming assets will definitely help to navigate the country away from impending austerity measures, the worst in the history of Nigeria. A blue print is available if the country is ready and willing to create millions of jobs for the youths.

There are many known ways to create bursts or economic booms in a nation or among a group of people. It just depends on what the powers that be are willing to use at any given point in time. The following methods of enslavement or boom and burst creation tools will be examined to see how they might translate to possibility of $125 or $25 barrel of crude oil price. Warfare, Crude Oil, Currency devaluation and Debt are the four major weapons that powerful groups and nations can use to enslave lesser groups or nations.

Warfare

These powers are the oldest and most cruel form of burst, suppression, submission and control that have been greatly used by powerful nations on weaker ones. In this modern age, that we are clouded with hidden cameras from every angle, warfare is rarely being used because of the horrifying images from the media houses. Nations and powerful groups are shying away from the use of warfare because the consequences are sometimes difficult to predict.

A case in point was the invasion of Kuwait by Iraq on 2nd August 1990 so they could have control of the crude oil rich country. The Iraqi invasion quickly drew gross condemnations from the global village. George .W. Bush, the then president of America, quickly assembled an international coalition against Iraq. On January 16th 1991 President George Bush addressed the U.N as follows; "Just 2 hours ago, allied air forces began an attack on military targets in Iraq and Kuwait. These attacks continue. As I speak. Ground forces are not engaged.

This military action, taken in accord with United Nations resolutions and with the consent of the United States Congress, followed months of constant and virtually endless diplomatic activity on the part of the United Nations, the United States, and many, many other countries. Arab leaders sought what became known as an Arab solution, only to conclude that Saddam Hussein was unwilling to leave Kuwait.

This conflict started August 2nd when the dictator of Iraq invaded a small and helpless neighbor. Kuwait, a member of the Arab League and a member of the United Nation, was crushed, and its people, brutalized. Five months ago, Saddam Hussein started this cruel war against Kuwait. Tonight, the battle has been joined.

Wow! See what mankind is willing to do all because of crude oil, invasions and counter-invasions? In our global social networked village of today, it is now becoming very difficult to use warfare as a tool of suppression and control because many in the global village today are reporters, thanks to Facebook, YouTube, twitter and the rest of the social media groups. Warfare requires the shedding of much innocent blood and often appeals to the emotions of by-standers. The unintended consequences are often deadly.

Crude Oil

The global village took a different dimension during the first week of August 1990 when Iraq invaded Kuwait. Crude oil prices immediately jumped to $30 a barrel from about a $22 a barrel trading range. That was about a 36% increase that quickly affected the prices of other consumers' basic daily needs such as the prices of gasoline, transportation, entertainment, food and other necessities of life. It caused them to go up drastically, creating huge cash outflow from the masses.

Crude oil is definitely an ideal tool for burst, boom or economic enslavement because once you sharply increase the price of crude oil, the nation and groups of people will definitely witness sharp or gradual increases in the prices of virtually everything. Inflation will set in and the economic cycle will start heading south into recession or depression if not quickly combated by the recipients. On the other hand the sharp selloff of crude oil prices would create a deflationary environment that would orchestrate an economic boom in any economy. Crude oil prices could be a more acceptable weapon of burst, suppression and economic enslavement to arrogantly or erroneously perceived nations or groups of people that are seen as a big threat to the global village.

Currency devaluation

For a currency to be devalued means that the issuing government has mandated that the exchange rate of the currency in relation to American dollar be lower than it was before. For example, if the Nigerian government changes the exchange rate from the current ₦200 (Naira) to $1, and suddenly moves the exchange rate to ₦240 (Naira) to $1, then the Naira has been devalued. Now, regardless of whether a country has a fixed or flexible exchange rate system, there exists a "true" equilibrium exchange rate. The equilibrium exchange rate is the exchange rate at which everyone who wants to sell currency can find a buyer and everyone who wants to buy currency can find a seller. By definition, a flexible exchange rate is the equilibrium exchange rate.

The author is mulishly bullish on the Naira exchange rate against American Dollar heading to ₦300 to $1 before the year 2015 runs out unless the government is willing to cut down the exorbitant recurrent expenditure by at least 50% and reduce government excess by a minimum of 35%.

President Muhammadu Buhari is a loving, disciplined, resilient, tenacious, and God fearing Nigerian who has the interest of the poor masses close to his heart. but until the masses give him unconditional support he will not be able to do much for the country because the legislative and judiciary arms of the government might frustrate his efforts. He definitely needs the masses on his side to be able to carry out any meaningful reform in the country.

A case in point was when Chris Ngige was first elected the governor of Anambra state (one of the states in the south). He could not do anything because his political godfathers wanted him to continue looting in the state. He blatantly refused and ran to the masses, who received and worked with him to make meaningful changes in the state. Chris Ngige's record still speaks volumes in Anambra state because he really impacted the lives of the poor masses.

Actually floating exchange rate is different from a fixed exchange rate where the government pegs the exchange rate of her currency, instead of allowing the true value of the currency to be determined by the market forces. Nonetheless, any country that by omission or commission devalued her currency would witness an immediate, sometimes prolonged and untold hardship to the masses because the purchasing power of her money has been quickly and greatly lowered. In some cases the masses can turn on their governments for letting such an event occur in their countries. In some cases, when a country devalues its currency, the country will probably follow it up with austerity measures such as cutting down on government spending, to make her goods and services relatively cheap to attract patronage from other nations.

However, in as much as devaluation could be an evil-oriented policy, countries that require a boom in their export businesses should seriously consider devaluing their currencies in order to make their goods and services have very attractive prices. When a nation devalues her currency, it makes the costs of her goods and services very attractive in relation to global village prices or her trading nations, and often times there will be gradual increase in the export trades of those countries that willingly or forcefully devalued their currencies. Nigeria and other African countries that export mainly crude oil would definitely not benefit from devaluing their currencies, because their economies are import-oriented and devaluations of any kind would be a double tragedy.

Debt

An amount owed to a person or organization for money borrowed could be in the form of loans, notes, bonds, mortgages or other stated transactions. You are a debtor when you owe someone and a creditor when someone else owes you. When you translate debt to a weapon of burst, suppression, containment and economic enslavement, you will understand why certain things are happening in the global village today. Perhaps the most creative form of manipulations and controls is debt because debt could be used in many ways to control, contain or suppress any individual, group or nation.

Countries that lack the spirit of teamwork, unity, huge debt, poor quality education, insufficient capital, and unproductiveness really needs big catalysts and global help to be the next engine of global growth. Nigeria unfortunately falls in that league of such nations. Foreign and local investors are so excited and looking forward to putting their money in Nigeria, but chances are very high that if the country's new government led by Muhammadu Buhari, a symbol of anti-corruption, fails to reduce the prevalent chronic corruption to mere corruption. Then all bets will be off the table. Nigeria really needs all the motivational encouragement and supports to win this war against chronic corruption or the country will quickly degenerate into uncharted territory.

After all is said and done, everything boils down to the direction the super powers want interest rates to go. Who will probably be the next victim? Will it be individual home-owners paying mortgages; those with outstanding student loans; over-leveraged countries like Greece, Spain, Portugal and many other third world countries. Debt weapon might actually be the most effective and efficient means of containment and control because human beings are naturally at the mercy of their creditors.

Meanwhile, there is still a large amount of crude oil in our global village, and until the excess supply dries up, crude oil will most likely get to $25 per barrel before bottoming out. This is the catalysts that will lead to the onslaught of crude oil demand. Destructions are being lined up, including solar powered cars, increasing use of robots in factories, battery powered cars, increasing use of natural gas, wind energy and the rest of pending inventions.

If you think that Nigeria and other African leaders are paying attention to all these changes, you better think again, because issues like, religious divide, tribal wars, militant groups, ethnic conflicts, boundary disputes, inflation, poor quality of education, human trafficking, chronic corruption, dysfunctional political and financial issues are keeping the leaders away from tinkering with global issues that might play out 10 to 15 years down the line.

Time is the biggest factor right now for Nigeria to prioritize her energy needs while diversifying her economy at the same time, because if the excess crude oil supply in the global village lingers much longer, then most of the crude oil producing nations would definitely find ways to increase their production quotas to make up for the less revenues coming into their treasuries. Crude oil, for many decades has dictated the direction of global economic growth because sharp huge rises in crude oil price will normally send the global economy in a recessionary mode, while sharp drop in price would create a deflationary mode. World primary energy consumption grew by 45% over the past 20 years, and is likely to grow by 39% over the next 20 years. Global energy consumption is projected to grow at an average of 1.7% p.a. from 2010 to 2030, with growth decelerating gently beyond 2020.

Non-OECD (Organization for Economic Development) energy consumption will be 68% higher by 2030, averaging 2.6% p.a. growth from 2010. It will account for 93% of global energy growth. OECD energy consumption in 2030 is projected to be just 6% higher than today, with growth averaging 0.3% p.a. to 2030. From 2020, OECD energy consumption per capita will be on a declining trend (-0.2% p.a.). The fuel mix changes will be at a relatively slow pace, due to long asset lifetimes. But gas and non-fossil fuels will gain share at the expense of coal and oil. The fastest growing fuels are renewable, including biofuels which are expected to grow at 8.2% p.a. by 2030. Among fossil fuels, natural gas grows the fastest (2.1% p.a.).

The three fossil fuels are approaching market shares of 26-27%. Meanwhile the major non-fossil fuel groups will have market shares of around 7% each. Oil continues to suffer a long run decline in market share, while gas steadily gains. Coal's recent gains in market share, on the back of rapid industrialization in China and India, would likely be reversed by 2030, since natural gas and solar energy technological efficiency continues to reduce the consumption of coal and crude oil.

The diversifying fuel mix can be seen most clearly in terms of contributions to growth. Over the period 1990-2010, fossil fuels contributed to 83% of the growth in energy; over the next twenty years, fossil fuels will contribute only 64% of the growth. Taken together, the contribution of all non-fossil fuels to growth over the next twenty years (36%) is, for the first time, larger than that of any single fossil fuel. Renewable energy, including biofuels will account for 18% of the growth in energy by 2030. The rate at which renewables penetrate the global energy market is similar to the emergence of nuclear power in the1970s and 1980s.

In the OECD energy consumption for transport is in decline and industrial use is likely to be flat. All the growth in energy end-use comes from the "other" sector (households and the service sector). In the non-OECD, industry drives the growth of final energy consumption, particularly in rapidly developing economies. Overall, energy used to generate power remains the fastest growing sector, accounting for 57% of the projected growth in primary energy consumption to 2030.

The diversification of the fuel mix is being driven largely by the power sector, where non-fossil fuels, led by renewable energies account for more than half of the growth. Gas accounts for more than half of the growth in fossil fuelled power. In transport, we are starting to see diversification, driven by policy and enabled by technology, with biofuels accounting for nearly a third of energy growth.

Strong growth in non-OECD energy consumption, especially of coal, translates into continued growth of global CO_2 emissions. The growth of global CO_2 emissions from energy averages 1.2% p.a over the next twenty years compared to 1.9% p.a. 1990-2010, leaving emissions in 2030 27% higher than today. The implementation of carbon abatement policies in the OECD will reduce the level of emissions in 2030, but only by 10% relative to current levels.

Non-OECD emissions are growing by 2.2% p.a. on average, up 53% by 2030. Policies in non-OECD countries focus on reducing the carbon intensity of economic growth. Carbon per unit of GDP will fall by 42% by 2030, and the rate of decline will accelerate steadily. By 2020-30, non- OECD emissions will grow by only 1.3% p.a., compared to 5.2% p.a. growth over 2000-2010

Overall, this implies some progress towards climate change goals, but not enough to put the world on a path to stabilization at 450 ppm. Oil is expected to be the slowest-growing fuel over the next 20 years. Global liquid demand for oil, biofuels, and other liquids nonetheless is likely to rise by 16.5 Mb/d, exceeding 102 Mb/d by 2030. Growth comes exclusively from rapidly-growing non-OECD economies. Non-OECD Asia accounts for more than three-quarters of the net global increase, rising by nearly 13 Mb/d. The Middle East and South & Central America will also grow significantly. OECD demand has likely peaked in 2005) and consumption is expected to decline by just over 4 Mb/d.

Rising supplies to meet or exceed the expected demand growth should come primarily from OPEC, where output is projected to rise by 13 Mb/d. The largest increments of new OPEC supply will come from NGLs, as well as conventional crude in Iraq and Saudi Arabia. Non-OPEC supply will continue to rise, albeit modestly. A large increase in biofuels supply, along with smaller increments from Canadian oil sands, deep-water Brazil, and the FSU should offset continued declines in a number of mature provinces.

Energy used for transport will continue to be dominated by oil, but should see its share of global energy use decline as other sectors grow more rapidly. Growth is expected to slow over the next twenty years to average 1.1% p.a. vs 1.8% p.a. during 1990-2010, with OECD demand slowing and then declining post-2015. The slowing of growth in total energy in transport is related to higher oil prices and improving fuel economy. Vehicle saturation in mature economies, is expected to increase taxation and subsidy reduction in developing economies.

The growth of oil in transportation slows even more dramatically, largely because of displacement of oil by biofuels and is likely to plateau in the mid-2020s. Currently, biofuels contribute 3% on an energy basis and are forecasted to rise to 9% at the expense of oil's share. Rail, electric vehicles, plug-in hybrids, and the use of compressed natural gas in transportation is likely to grow, but without making a material contribution to total transportation before 2030.

China is the largest source of oil consumption growth in our outlook, with consumption forecast to grow by 8 Mb/d to reach 17.5 Mb/d by 2030, overtaking the US to become the world's largest oil consumer. Growth is expected to remain concentrated in the industrial and transport sectors through 2020. Industrial growth slows post-2020 as industrial expansion becomes less energy intensive and population growth slows; transportation will then be the dominant driver of growth. Despite contributing almost half of net global oil consumption growth by 2030, there is a projection of a slower increase in per capita consumption than seen historically in other Asian economies. China is much less dependent on oil in its overall fuel mix (20%) than many other emerging economies at similar points in their development. In addition, China is likely to implement policies to slow oil consumption growth, such as increasing taxes on transport fuels and maximizing use of other fuels. Oil prices are higher than faced historically by other emerging economies, and rising import dependence is a policy concern.

Globally liquids production is expected to increase to meet the growth in consumption, though the sources of growth will change the global balance. Global liquids supply is set to rise by about 16.5 Mb/d by 2030. OPEC accounts for over 75% of global supply growth, with OPEC NGLs expected to grow by more than 4 Mb/d, driven in part by rapid growth of natural gas production. Iraqi crude output is projected to grow from about 2.5 Mb/d currently to more than 5.5 Mb/d. Saudi output is likely to expand by nearly 3 Mb/d.

Non-OPEC output will rise by nearly 4 Mb/d. Unconventional supply growth should more than offset declining conventional output, with bio- fuels adding nearly 5 Mb/d and oil sands rising by nearly 2 Mb/d. Declining conventional crude supply in Europe, Asia Pacific and North America is partly offset by growth in deep-water Brazil and the FSU, resulting in a net decline of just over 3 Mb/d. In this outlook Russia and Saudi Arabia will each sustain their current market share of roughly 12% over the next 20 years.

The importance of OPEC is expected to grow. In our projections, OPEC's share of global production would increase from 40% in 2010 to 46% in 2030, a level not reached since 1977. In the early years of the outlook, OPEC production growth can be met by utilizing current spare capacity. Over time capacity must expand to meet expected growth demand. In addition to NGL growth, we project an increase in crude oil production capacity of nearly 5 Mb/d by 2030 – to nearly 40 Mb/d – largely in Iraq and Saudi Arabia.

These projections imply that Saudi production capacity, currently at 12.5 Mb/d, is likely to be sufficient to meet demand and maintain a reasonable buffer of spare capacity until around 2020. Thereafter, a modest expansion appears likely. While we do not attempt to forecast long-term energy prices, the ability and willingness of OPEC members to expand capacity and production is clearly one of the main factors determining the path of the oil market.

Natural gas is projected to be the fastest growing fossil fuel globally through 2030, but slows relative to historic patterns as the market base expands and -supply side measures gain hold. Production grows in every region except Europe, where decline rates at mature fields are likely to reverse the gains since 1975. Asia accounts for the world's largest production and consumption increments. China drives 56% of the region's consumption growth.

The Middle East has the world's second largest production and consumption increments. The region's share in global consumption is expected to expand from 5% in1990and 12% in 2010 to 17% in 2030. Its share in global production grows from 15% in 2010 to 19%.Despite North America's continued production growth. It is quite obvious that North America will be outpaced by other regions. I Its share in the global total will decline from 26% in 2010 to 19% by 2030.

The summary of all the above report figures points to possible $125 or $25 a barrel of crude in the near future. If mankind can globally bring down the costs of renewable and other alternative energy before we can know the true position of crude oil reserves, then the global village might likely see $25 a barrel for crude oil first. On the contrary, if we get the true position of our global crude oil reserve with high costs of renewable and other alternative energy, then the global village will say a big hello to $125 a barrel of crude oil.

There is high possibility that global crude oil reserves were well overstated to give mankind time to find an alternative energy that will power the paradigm shift. Believe it or not, mankind is in a big race to save our scarce resources and prolong the doomsday from our once friendly climate.

America's recent space mission to aggressively probe planet Mars may have confirmed the true state of mankind's desperation from our climate threats. Global teamwork is all that is required now to put mankind ahead of the destructive curve of end times. The technological break-through in solar, wind and engineering efficiency has given mankind solid advantage over coal and crude oil, but the race is still on to reduce the cost of solar energy which is available in excess. It is becoming obvious that the combination of natural gas, solar energy and increasing advance in technology will eventually relegate the use of coal and crude oil to make our environment safer.

CHAPTER 9

Navigating through the Worst Austerity Measures

After the global depression of the 1930s, 44 countries under a United Nations (UN) conference in Bretton Woods, New Hampshire America wanted to prevent such future economic disaster conceived a frame work called International Monetary Fund (IMF) also known as the fund. The participants believed that the great depression was caused by global competitive devaluations of currencies, so in July of 1944, IMF came into existence. The primary goal of IMF was to ensure the stability of international monetary system—the system of exchange rates that enables countries and their citizens to transact businesses and inter-countries business transactions too. In 2012, the objective was updated to include all macroeconomic and financial sector issues that bear on global stability.

IMF's main types of work are as follows: Surveillance, Lend and Technical assistance

Surveillance: To monitor economic and financial developments in all member countries and provide policy advice aimed at preventing future economic and financial catastrophes in any of the countries.

Lend: To quickly advance and lend money, provide temporary financing, and support member policies aimed at correcting underlying problems that caused the financial distress in member countries. Loans to under-developing countries were aimed at reducing poverty in member countries.

Technical Assistance: To provide technical assistance and training in its areas of expertise to member countries. IMF was supposed to play an important role in the fight against money laundering and terrorism also. An overview of IMF towards Nigeria and other African countries clearly indicate that its policies urgently need to be restructured because billions of dollars are being siphoned out of the continent every year. The world would love to know if IMF failures in Nigeria and other African countries were as result of chronic corruption in the continent, wrong analysis of the continent's problems or using unqualified personnel in the continent. IMF has to do more in Africa because the failed policies in the continent would eventually constitute serious economic and financial nightmares to the global village.

Austerity Measures (AM) could be defined as painful and strict measures that are undertaken by a government to help bring capital and recurrent expenditures more in line with revenues.

Austerity Measures could be voluntarily implemented by a sovereign government to restructure and redirect its economy into a sustainable path. On the other hand, austerity measures might also be forced down on a sovereign nation if the country defaults on its debt obligations and want to borrow more from World Bank or International Monetary Fund (IMF). Whether it is called Austerity measures or Structural Adjustment Programs (SAP), they are both interchangeably used with the same expected outcomes, but unfortunately, these programs are more complex for Nigeria and other African countries. The programs have never worked well in this continent, because of chronic corruption that hampers the recommended structural reforms.

Nigeria and other African countries implemented series of Structural Adjustment Programs in the 1980s and before the programs could come to fruition, chronic corruption surged and destroyed everything including the little gains made from the programs. Now what would be the reason for asking Nigeria and other African leaders to embrace Structural Adjustment Programs again without first addressing the issues of chronic corruption in the continent?

Can these programs work in less corruption infested countries? Sure! Just that the high level of chronic corruption in Nigeria and other African countries will always kill anything, whether it's Austerity Measures or Structural Adjustment Programs, they can only work where there is system of checks and balances.

Jimi Hendrix once said "When the power of love overcomes the love of power, the world will know peace. Please show some love to Nigeria, now that Nigeria is really in the need of help and has elected a person, Muhammadu Buhari, who has a wonderful track record of fighting corruption. Nigeria will be asked to embrace austerity measures in a matter of months because past Nigerian political leaders failed to pre-empt the long term effects of chronic corruption and the demand destructions in crude oil to the economy. Chronic corruption and falling crude oil prices are speedily eating up the country's revenues and foreign reserves. That would make it impossible for the country to service her debts in the near future. Expect the International Monetary Fund (IMF) and World Bank to invite Nigerian finance minister to discuss ways of helping the country to honor her debt obligations.

It is so obvious that the issue of austerity measures would be on the table because Nigeria's borrowing power has drastically gone down. At the same time the country definitely needs to borrow to service her debts. Nigerians should be reminded that the country's deficit spending has been increasingly going up ever since crude oil prices left the $100 per barrel mark, Thus those Nigerians hoping to see the new president Muhammadu Buhari perform magic would be disappointed. Unless, 90% of Nigerian looted treasury is recovered, the president and his team would not have enough money to carry out his campaign manifesto. This is where Nigerians could decide a way forward. Maybe some of the kind hearted politicians might offer to return some of their loot to save Nigeria, because head or tail, Nigeria must go through another difficult time in the coming months.

Meanwhile, let us take a closer look at these theories to understand what austerity measures are all about. Before the uninformed Nigerians would start labeling IMF and World Bank as evil institutions They need to realize that chronic corruption destroyed Nigeria and not either of the institutions. The poor masses watched as the nation's treasury was being looted from all corners and helplessly could not do much to stop the worst treasury looting in the history of the country. The Keynes vs. Hayek Theories arguments are as follows:

The Keynes vs. Hayek Debate

John Maynard Keynes and Friedrich Hayek were two famous economists with differing opinions on how to address the boom bust cycle that leads to budget deficits. In fact, the debates between these two economists were somewhat famous for being rather lively and rowdy.

Keynes argued that governments should intervene to help put the jobless back to work by implementing economic stimulus and other programs. He argued that if these people were employed, GDP growth would accelerate and debt as a percentage of GDP would be reduced. The prospects of a long-term growth rate would also make financing current projects much easier and growth will escalate.

Hayek insisted that these programs would simply setback the day of reckoning. Instead, he argued that the governments should instead reduce spending and taxes in order to make room for the free market to determine the right course of action. He admitted that while the government cutting spending and taxes could mean increased painful hardship in the short-term, the gains would equate to a far healthier long-term and sustainable economy.

Both economists are actually right in their view points. But those theories were only designed to work in structured political and economic environments, and not unstructured political and economic environments that are overly infested with chronic corruption, no bonding common interests from ethnic groups and increasing deficit spending. It is quite obvious that neither theory would work in this country unless the country quickly addresses the issue of chronic corruption. Unless they do laudable programs or measures will never yield the desired result.

An average Nigerian can now understand why the new president said "Nigeria must kill corruption or corruption will kill Nigeria". Not fighting chronic corruption from all corners should not even be an option to consider if the country still wants to remain relevant in the global village. History of failures in Nigeria and other African countries should not be traced to those economic models because chronic corruption would not let anything work in the continent. The only political and economic model that can work in Nigeria and other African countries now will be an aggressive "War against Corruption (WAC)". When this battle of corruption is conquered by Nigerians with reasonable amount of help from other global villagers, then either of the economic models of Keynes or Hayek will work in Nigeria.

The IMF and the World Bank should prescribe a high dose of WAC to all corruption-ridden countries like Nigeria and other under developing countries before giving such countries loans. Otherwise, it will be just a repeat of vicious cycles and wasted rescue efforts.

Evil can never beget good, and good can never ever beget evil. Let the global village help Nigeria and other under-developing countries to eradicate chronic corruption in their countries, because chronic corruption kills more than terrorist groups. Chronic corruption and terrorist groups are anti economic and financial growths and the global village should join forces and address those issues decisively.

Austerity measures or Structural Adjustment Programs usually include massive governments' spending cuts, currency devaluation, subsidies' withdrawals and tax increases. Suffice it to say that all the above requirements of Austerity measures are absolutely not human friendly, yet human beings are corruptly blinded not to avoid these deadly requirements of Austerity measures, by curbing chronic corruption in their countries. The genesis of implementing Austerity measures can sometimes be traced to resource mismanagement, unplanned global economic/financial events, and poorly prepared budgets., But the chief foundational cause of implementing Austerity measures in Nigeria, is a high level of chronic corruption.

Resource mismanagements

Resource mismanagement occurs in virtually all parts of the global village, but since many under-developing countries lack the discipline to institute appropriate systems of "Check and Balances", the negative effects of resource mismanagements tend to be more devastating in poor and developing countries like Nigeria. The predominant number of countries engulfed in resource mismanagement could be found in Africa because of high level of chronic corruption in the public sector. After the global crude oil boom in the late 1979s to early 1980s African countries including Nigeria squandered the enormous financial excess they received in the era of the crude oil boom through high level of corruption. And shortly after squandering the resources they turned around and accumulated so much debt, from excessive borrowing and currency devaluation. As soon as Nigeria and other African leaders exhausted the accumulated excess revenues from high crude oil prices, they went to IMF for more borrowing forgetting that their borrowing power has drastically decreased. As the saying goes "He who pays the piper dictates the tones". The corrupt Nigerian and African leaders had to accept the unfriendly conditions of the loans, because they needed to fund so fast to satisfy their embezzlement appetite in the continent.

Since man is a political animal that refuses to learn why deadly preventable events happen, very soon, Nigeria and other African leaders would be rushing to World Bank and International Monetary Fund (IMF) for more borrowing. Maybe Nigeria should be excluded this time around because of the new president's tenacity in fighting corruption, but would Nigerians give him unconditional support to kill chronic corruption, before it kills Nigeria?

Suffice it to say that if the new president fails to kill chronic corruption, then the nation must be rescued by the unfriendly loan terms of IMF and World Bank. The saying that 'History will always find a way of repeating itself" is technically true, because it seems that Nigeria is at the verge of repeating history.

Whatever happened in Nigeria in 1984 that first brought Muhammadu Buhari and his team into the political arena to save the country has gotten worse now. But this time around, the tenacious president has a mandate of the majority of Nigerians and the team of anointed men of God to accomplish the task.

The first time Muhammadu Buhari mantled the leadership of this country in mid 1980s, the politicians had already infested the entire country with chronic corruption. The few months he was in power, he set a system in motion to fight chronic corruption, and Nigeria was beginning to move in the right direction when his government suddenly was overthrown and chronic corruption returned and surged unabated. Does it really mean that human beings are very ignorant of their own history? Why would human beings, who are the master-piece creation of God, forget so soon? People that are ignorant of their own history will always face serious challenges that might lead to their disintegration. When people refuse to learn and study their past mistakes, they tend to forget, and when they forget, the mistakes are often repeated in a greater magnitude.

Nonetheless, the accepted World Bank and IMF borrowing terms and conditions to Nigeria gave birth to austerity measures that devastated the expanding and gradually developing Nigerian economy. As if Nigerian political leaders are slow in learning from their past mistakes, because all the economic indicators are currently pointing towards failure.

Unless Nigerians collectively fight chronic corruption, history is about to repeat in the country. Actually, the saying that "History will always repeats itself" is technically pointing towards the fact because Nigeria and many other Sub-Saharan African countries are about to be enveloped in another waves of borrowings from IMF that would require the implementation of austerity measures.

 Austerity measures/Structural Adjustment Programs have no human face and should not be prescribed to countries that are soaked in high levels of chronic corruption. Saying that austerity measures terms are technically bad for countries with high level of chronic corruption does not mean it is evil. It should work perfectly well in structured economies with lesser degrees of corruption, like Greece, Spain, Portugal and France, therefore, unless a nation reduces the level of chronic corruption, austerity measures should not be prescribed to that country.

Unplanned global economic/financial events

The unintended consequences of the American Federal Reserve withdrawing quantitative easing and the probable start of increasing interest rates in the country will result in global rising interest rates. And developing and under-developing economies never perform well in a global rising interest rate era. One of the reasons being, since interest rate charges are already high in Nigeria and other African countries due to chronic corruption, the global rise in interest rates normally would create severe financial imbalance and economic disenfranchisement to such countries.

The global village is currently enjoying low interest rates environment because European Union embarked on her own version of quantitative easing in early 2015. However, the threat of inflation might invariable force the American fed to change the language that is keeping the interest rates down, or just start the gradual interest rate increases. Ordinarily, the American fed has no business increasing the fed fund rate because low interest rates helps the real estate sector of the economy, and American dollar is performing very strong against other major currencies. The over performance of the American dollar against other major currencies has resulted in many American companies generating a certain percentage of the revenues reporting quarterly losses, so if the Fed increases the fed fund rate very soon, that might not be a wise idea.

When a nation's currency is not performing very well (losing exchange values against other currencies), there are some very important steps that such country must take to shore up the value of her currency such as increase the federal fund rate, eliminate chronic corruption, increase export trades and increase productivity;

Increase fed fund rate

When a nation's currency starts to quickly lose the exchange rate value and purchasing power against other major currencies, one of the measures to be taken by the Apex bank of such country to correct such abnormal occurrence would be for the Apex bank to start increasing the federal fund rates. That will, in turn increase the cost of borrowing in the country, thereby reducing the excess liquidity. In any structured economy, such a move would definitely help to shore up the value of a currency and increase the currency purchasing power.

But in country like Nigeria where the surging under-ground economy is growing faster than the real economy, such monetary policy likely would not work because so much money from chronic corruption activities is constantly being injected into the real economy negating the Apex bank's effort to reverse the falling trend of the currency. Nigerian CBN governor Dr. Godwin Emefele attempted that antidote to save Naira, but it did not work because chronic corruption was working behind the scenes and working around the clock.

Eliminate chronic corruption

Regardless of the monetary or fiscal policies put in place to help rescue the fast falling currency value, such policies might just be a temporary measure, because chronic corruption will eventually kill such measures. In 1981, the Nigerian Naira was being exchanged against American dollar at the rate of N0.52 to $1. Look at what chronic corruption has done to Nigerian currency. It is now at the current exchange rate of ₦200 to $1 in a span of 34 years. One thing is definitely certain about the Nigerian choice of what to do. If chronic corruption cannot be eliminated in the country, the Naira might definitely head to ₦300, and then ₦500 to $1. From the past performance of the Naira against the American dollar, it is quite obvious that Nigerians not joining the government to fight chronic corruption would not be an acceptable option because chronic corruption is about to deal a total losing hand to the country. The masses must collectively help the new president win the battle of chronic corruption or else their tomorrow will be far worse than their today.

Increase export trades

Increasing the trade export of a country would help to shore up the value of a falling currency, because everything about our lives center on supply and demand. Increasing the level of exporting activities in a country that is rapidly losing the purchasing power of her currency would reduce the demand for other currencies for importation of goods and services into the country.

Humans are always quick to underestimate the powerful forces of supply and demand because any attempt to control the demand appetite without adequate supply would definitely result in a catastrophic situation to that nation. Nigeria's new administration really has to spend enough resources on promoting non-crude oil exports. That is why it is very imperative that developing ports to advanced levels and including some of the professional super-stars on the export lists, will help the country to ease the pains of austerity measures that is dangerously imminent.

Increase productivity

Increasing the productivity of a country like Nigeria is one of the best ways of strengthening the purchasing value of the Naira, because when a nation consumes more than what could be produced, the nation has to import to make up for the difference. Nigeria imports virtually everything from common toothpicks to even the processed crude oil the country has in abundance. Only supernatural intervention would make the currency of the country to gain value against other major currencies in the global village. Nigeria is currently in a precarious economic and financial position, because the country exports crude oil for less and pays more to import the processed crude oil. Nigerian refineries can barely processes up to 30% of the country's consumption, so the difference has to be imported putting double pressure on the country's currency.

Nigerians should not pay attention to an unverified comment that the new administration would get down the exchange rate of the Naira against the American dollar at the rate of ₦100 for $1 within a year, economists would really love to see this happen, but if wishes were horses, then beggars would ride. The president is known to the global village as a good chronic corruption fighter and a liberal man that is willing to help the poor masses but he is not known as a magician that can make the illusionary acts become realty. Nigerians could not have gotten a better president to try to salvage the country, but if Nigerians expect him to perform magic, then the masses would be in for rude awakening because he cannot meet their demands. If the country can be saved, Nigerians have the best pilot (the world does not know anything about the crew members) to give air Nigeria a perfect soft landing. Nonetheless the pilot must receive unconditional support from both the crew members and the masses to soft land the air Nigeria that is speedily losing altitude.

Unplanned global economic/financial events can also force visionary and proactive countries to voluntarily implement austerity measures and soften the costly and negative consequences orchestrated from such events. Just like what happened in many European Nations When in the 2008 global financial melt-down and credit crunch that originated from the great American economy threw the global village into panic and shock. When the melt down started ravaging the economies of many E.U (European Union) countries that failed to quickly react to the global financial melt-down, many nations were left licking their wounds.

Repeated series of social media warnings to Nigerian leaders to preempt the looming negative effects of austerity measures in the country fell on deaf ears, because the leaders were warned to conserve the fast depleting foreign reserves, and no action was taken. Greece, Spain, Portugal and host of other European countries are battling the socio-political effects of economic and financial consequences of implementing Austerity measures.

Nigerian leaders once again must prepare and make adequate plans on how to deal with the projected 2015 massive implementations of austerity measures in Nigeria and other African countries. This might also challenge the fabrics of co-existence in many member nations, because countries are more likely to embrace contracting instead of the much needed expansionary economy that would accommodate the high number of unemployed Nigerians. The author is mulishly bullish in predicting that the impending austerity Measures in Nigeria and other African countries will result in another wave of elevated scrambling out of Nigeria and other African countries by Nigerians and other Africans to other part of the global village while the new colonial masters will quietly sneak into Nigeria and the continent.

What is happening in South Africa today is actually a prelude to what is going to happen in many other African countries. It is a sign of looming austerity measures, because African leaders have gotten through looting all the treasuries and they are now looking to see whom to blame for their reckless and looting appetite. If Nigerian and other African leaders had not embezzled the resources that could have been used to create jobs in their respective countries, you would not have seen all these many Africans fighting with South Africans over the little available jobs in their country.

African leaders should be held accountable for what is going on in South Africa today. Violence is not good so the ignorant South Africans should start asking their leaders questions on what is going on in their economy and not blaming the poor foreigners that are only trying to make ends meet. Sometime in the 1980s, when the political class emptied the country's treasure, jobs were had to come by because austerity measures were gradually setting into the country. Nigerians angrily sent Ghanaians away from Nigeria, claiming that the Ghanaians were taking away their jobs. If every country decides to send foreigners away from their countries, it might be very difficult to see a country that would be left standing.

Poorly prepared budgets

Every year, Nigeria spends millions of Naira to prepare budgets that never get to see daylight. Either the budgets were poorly prepared or reasonable projections were never made by those that prepared the budgets. The Nigerian budget for year 2015 was changed more than three times because of speedily falling crude oil price, and yet the budget does not look feasible. Chances are very high that by end of the year, the budget might not be used. Maybe Nigerian policy makers are grossly underestimating the importance of a well prepared budget, or that chronic corruption plays a major role in budgeting process.

Poorly prepared budgets that failed to reasonably predict, forecast and make adequate provisions for predictable future occurrences will always make any sovereign government leader a frequent customer to IMF and World Bank borrowings. Austerity measures can never take place in any nation, unless resources of such nation were grossly mismanaged or occurrence of natural disaster that causes a huge financial outlay. In cases where there are reasonably prepared budgets, chronic corruption will hamper the implementations of such budgets and make mockery of the budgetary efforts, by the professionals that have spent hours preparing the budgets.

Unfortunately, the high levels of chronic corruption in Nigeria has made it virtually impossible for many governments' projects to be completed without repeated re-awarding of the projects or in some cases abandoning such projects. Chronic corruption has made it possible for bribes to be indirectly acceptable in many governments' ministries to receive a 10% kickback (a chronic corruption fee) for any government project that must be awarded to an entity.

Competence and experience are no longer relevant in Nigerian governments awarding of projects. Once the corruption fee has been paid, the contract will be awarded. From the look of all things, one can reasonably ascertain that until chronic corruption is aggressively reduced to minimally acceptable level, any project instituted in the country will have short and unsustainable pattern of success because such project will not be vetted based on merit, rather on corruption oriented bids and ethnic and tribal basis.

Nigerians cannot build a strong and formidable country with the level of chronic corruption and division among major ethnic groups in the country. Eliminating chronic corruption must be the top priority of the new administration in order to move the country forward. Nation building requires less corruption and teamwork among the builders. Anything less than teamwork and limited corruption will definitely derail the builder's tenacity to efficiently accomplish the task. The new president is definitely a good builder, but would his co-builders have the same liberal minds to get the country to start moving towards greatness?

Based on the conviction that corruption has deeply eaten Nigeria to the fabrics of the foundations that held the country together, the third quarter of 2015 might witness uncontrollable surge in the number of kidnapping cases, armed robbery cases and socio-political events as Nigeria struggles to implement austerity measures/Structural Adjustment Programs, in an effort to save the country. Nigerians have to collectively make sacrifices, stand behind the new president and his team in order to save the country from the clear and immediate danger of politically self-induced severe hardship from all the past leaders. There is absolutely no doubt that Nigeria will rise up again as a force to be globally reckoned with, if only Nigerians would be willing to make the painful sacrifices that are required to power the country to greatness.

Let us take a look at some of the effects of Austerity measures

Economic Effects: Many aggregate demand models in economics suggest a relatively simple relationship between a government's budget and economic activity. That is, austerity measures lead to reduced consumptions, increase in export activities, reduction in importations, devalued currencies, higher unemployment rates, and increased economic output.

Reduced consumptions: Once the currency of a nation that implements austerity measures gets devalued, goods and services becomes very, very expensive and the number of citizens that can afford the goods and services becomes few. Many states were already having problems trying to pay the minimum salary of ₦18,000 per month prior to CBN voluntary devaluation from ₦165 to ₦199 per $1. So image what would be the fate of majority of Nigerian workers at the current exchange rate of ₦204 to $1, less than $100 a month. The majority of Nigerians simply became poorer by that CBN monetary policy of devaluing the currency. Please do not blame CBN because that was the hand the political class dealt to the apex bank by running the most expensive and unproductive government in the world. Few Nigerians cannot afford to eat even two square meals in a day. Consumption rate of virtually everything in the country is going drastically down.

Increase in export activities: This is one of the major advantages of austerity measures because the devalued currency will make the country's goods and services very attractive to foreign buyers. Non- productive countries like under developed ones really have fewer advantages to implement austerity measures because such countries lack the required technologies to perfect their goods and services. Nigeria and many other African countries are consuming nations. So embracing austerity measures should be least of their worries. They will now spend more of their monies to get fewer goods and services from the international community.

If Nigerian government can start purging herself of all the excess waste in running the government, and use the saving to aggressively promote export trades, then the country would definitely benefit in the long run. All developing and under-developed countries should channel more resources towards fighting the high levels of chronic corruption that are eating them alive before accepting IMF and World Bank loans. They should let the bulk of the loans be used in promoting export trades.

Reduction in importations: This might be considered as an advantage or disadvantage depending on the side you are. When a nation's currency gets devalued, buying imported goods and services becomes very expensive and citizens really want to buy locally manufactured goods and services. But the problem is that Nigeria operates an import-oriented economy where most of the products Nigerians consume are imported. Devaluation of the Naira will cause huge demand resulting in inflationary effects in the country because more money will now be chasing fewer locally manufactured goods and services. The majority of the poor Nigerian working class families that have not been paid for some time, maybe 3 months, will have to shop at the same markets where the politicians that can afford all those goods and services shop. Not supporting the new administration to conquer chronic corruption should not be an option for a true Nigerian. The poor masses have to really take control of their future by throwing their unconditional support behind the new president and his team to eradicate chronic corruption in the country.

Devalued currencies: Devaluation of any nation's currency tend to have negative impact on the lives of the citizens both short term and long term, except in developed and structured economies where the devaluation will gradually increase such country's export numbers and at the same time, create many opportunities in export related jobs. The increase in productivity of such country will be compensated with adequate salary increases from surging manufacturing jobs. If Nigeria cannot conquer chronic corruption, level the ground for industrialization to surge and embark on aggressive export promotions, then the Naira should not be devalued any further, because chronic corruption will likely erode any anticipated gain.

Higher unemployment rates: Nigeria and under-developing nations' devaluing their currencies really does not benefit those nations much, because the underlying problems of under development are not being address. The austerity measures that Nigeria embraced in the 1980s would have gotten the country moving towards the path of greatness, but unfortunately, chronic corruption that was the prevailing problem then was grossly overlooked.

Those countries like Nigeria, are still under developed primarily because of chronic corruption, and encouraging such countries to accept austerity measures or structural adjustment programs without conquering the root cause of the problem will definitely further devastate such economies. The global village would want to know of any African country that has successfully implemented austerity measures in the past that is now better off today because chronic corruption will eventually destroy virtually everything.

Nigerians must unite and face chronic corruption which is the country's common enemy and failure to win the war against chronic corruption will degenerate the country into uncharted territory, which outcome might be so painful to all Nigerians. Let Nigerians chase substance instead of shadow. The IMF and the World Bank should seriously consider forcing any African country coming to borrow funds to first eliminate chronic corruption and aggressively monitor how such funds will be deployed in their respective countries. Anything short of the above suggestion will be gross injustice towards the poor masses.

Increased economic output: Implementation of austerity measures may actually come with increase economic output in some developing and under-developing economies, but major advantages will be in structured and developed economies where companies would have many incentives to employ more labor and increase their export quotas. Where would these developing and under developed countries get the much needed capital to expand their economies? The majority of under-developed countries like Nigeria are running the most expensive and wasteful style of government, and any borrowed fund would wind up in recurrent expenditures leaving literally nothing for capital expenditures.

However, some other studies suggest that the relationship between austerity measures and economic activity is nonlinear and depend on many outside factors, which make these effects uncertain. In highly corruption infested countries, as witnessed in many developing and under developed economies, austerity measures can never work effectively because chronic corruption will eat up the gains that come with the programs.

Political Effects: Aside from monetary and fiscal effects, austerity measures can have a number of effects on a country's politics. Since most austerity measures target subsidies' withdrawals, increasing tax collections, and cutting of socially oriented spending, social unrests, high unemployment rates, increases in criminal and fraudulent activities will definitely pose another challenge to the government in power. Sometimes, a nation implementing austerity measures would witness uncontrollable surge in prices of goods and services, capital outflow, surge in under-ground economy, etc. Actually these are some of the unintended consequences of austerity measures.

Implementing austerity measures in any country will also tend to increase the political uncertainty in that country, because foreign investors would rather be on the sideline to see how the charged polity will cool down. Advice to Nigeria and other African countries that are having growth problems, would be to curb chronic corruption, reduce excess government wastes and efficiently manage the foreign reserves, because if you fail, then you must swallow the IMF and World Bank's bitter pills of austerity measures. Save your country the deadly and aggravating pains of forced austerity measures, by simply engaging in good governance and shying away from chronic corruption.

Social Effects: An increase in criminal activities as some of the individuals that lost their jobs will now join the underground economic activities that increase the insecurity problems in the country. Cases of armed robberies, fraudsters, kidnappings will be on an alarming increase, because more people would now be unemployed, and those that are working would be taking home devalued currency that only purchases a few goods. Many students whose parents cannot afford the increased fees will probably join men of the underground world or join cult groups and eventually come back to unleash deadly crimes in the country.

Austerity measures are implemented in order to cut federal deficits that can cripple a government's ability to finance its operations and repay any outstanding debt obligation. However, there are two other methods that can also be used to address federal deficits. Nigeria and other African countries have records of running the most expensive and wasteful style of governments in the global village, by reducing the huge costs of running such governments, one would have saved African governments billions of dollars that were lavishly spent on those big governments. Nigerians and other Africans will not want to pay taxes because they do not feel that their governments are properly representing them. If Nigerians and other Africans can jointly unite and aggressively fight chronic corruption in the continent, Africa will be on the path for another great success stories.

The global village need to make it the number one priority to encourage, motivate and if need be, force Nigeria and other African leaders to urgently start the War Against Corruption (WAC) programs, if not, the population of Africa might be listed as endanger species, and will be put in UN United Nation's conservative and lives' preserving lists. Global village should not forget that chronic corruption in Africa were one of the tools used by colonial masters in conquering African countries, all hands should now be on deck to purge chronic corruption from the continent, because it is devastating Africans. Chronic corruption has gone beyond individual country like Nigeria to conquer; the help of countries like America and other European Nations are highly needed to curb a deadly menace that is speedily killing millions of Nigerians and other Africans.

For the love of many innocent Nigerian children, the global village should by all means help to promote transparencies in Nigeria, by encouraging, sensitizing, and publicly commending good leadership in the country. Yes! Nigeria has the potential of becoming the next engine of global growth, but if the leaders continue to mismanage the country's depleting resources at such a speedy rate, where would the capital to make the country attractive to foreign investors come from? Needless to say that if the new Muhammadu Buhari government refuses to embrace reforms that would encourage the much needed capital inflows into the country, then Nigerians should be ready to expect whatever evil that might befall the country.

Meanwhile, expanding Nigerian Stock Market Exchange, empowering towns/villages in power sharing equation, using sports to unite tribal groups, addressing the land use acts, and aggressively fighting chronic corruption might be very helpful in reducing the negative economic and financial impacts that would befall the country from the impending austerity measures. Doing nothing by the new administration would definitely not be an acceptable option, because the danger is clear and immediate.

Henceforth, Nigerians should not expect too much from Muhammadu Buhari's government because he has to figure out a crafty way to get out from all the vultures that are thoughtfully hovering around him now. Those vultures are heavy loads and they can never allow the president to fulfill the pledge he made to Nigerians, really the president definitely needs the masses understanding, prayers, patience and minimal pressures to help discharge the political vultures and recover some of the loots. Nigerians must be mentally ready and willing to patiently work with the new president because the journey to eradicate chronic corruption and restore the economy will be a very long and tiring one due to the following constraints; Chinese slowing economic growth rate, Nigerian growing debts, Unrealistic value of Naira, Nigerian big and wasteful government, decaying infrastructures and austerity measures

Chinese slowing economic growth rate

China's slowing economic growth might have adverse effect in Nigerian economy because China is one of the country's biggest trading partners. For the past five years, China's economic growth rate has been sequentially slowing down and since it is the biggest buyer of Nigerian crude oil, they are likely to reduce the quantity they buy from Nigeria and at the same time reduce or stop credit facilities the commercial banks had extended to Nigerians. Some of the institutional and retail investors from China might also reduce their investment portfolios in the country, resulting in another wave of capital outflows.

Nigerian growing debts

Ever since the price of crude oil has dropped below $77 per barrel, the country's deficit spending has been mounting, so by the time Nigerians realize how much their external and internal debts are, IMF might be asking the country to devalue the already beaten up poor Naira. Rising debts and slowing economic growth rate is actually a nightmare for a developing country like Nigeria. If the poor masses can endure the impending hardship and work with the new administration, Nigeria will be up and running in some years to come.

Unrealistic value of Naira

the current exchange rate of Naira today (₦200 to $1) is definitely not the true value of the currency. Expect Naira to find an equilibrium exchange value against the American dollar when, the government stop fixing the rate. The masses should not point fingers at the new administration when they wake up one day and see exchange rate of about ₦300 to $1. So many damages had been done to Nigerian economy in the past, and the author expects those damages to start playing out when the new government takes office. Since 2007 when American Federal Reserve started to devalue American dollar to help the country increase her export rate in the global village, all major currencies were appreciating against American dollar except the Nigerian Naira, now that American economy is firing from all cylinders, king Dollar has been surging against all the currencies except Naira again.

Nigerian big and wasteful government

Nigerian government is one of the biggest and wasteful government systems in the world, and if allows to stay the way is, please do not expect any meaningful growth in the country. When the recurrent expenditures takes up about 75% of the annual budget, what then is left for capital expenditures that would help to create jobs in the country. Good a thing, the new government has indicated interest in cutting down the wasteful government.

Decaying infrastructures

The new government must quickly cut down the recurrent expenditures and ploy the money into rebuilding and building new infrastructures in the country, because any $1 that the government spends in building infrastructures will indirectly return about $10 to the government down the line. Building infrastructures in the country will create some jobs at the same time. The money recovered from looting and excess recurrent expenditures quickly need to go into building infrastructures in the country because it will also increase workers productivity.

Austerity measures

It is quite unfortunate that Nigerians must have to go through this unfriendly event again because of the looting that took place in the country for so many years. Chronic corruption must be eradicated from the country to make sure that Nigeria would not go through this again. The most important lesson from the impending austerity measure would be for Nigerians to collectively join forces to eradicate chronic corruption from the country, and this is the only way the country can move forward.

Are Nigerians ready to make the required painful sacrifices that are absolutely needed to transform the country from among the most corrupt countries of the world to a new Nigeria the entire world would be praising for 360 degree of positive turn around? Sometimes, human beings find ways to draw strength from their weaknesses and colossal mistakes; can Nigerians partake in drawing strength from the social, political, financial and economic mistakes that would unleash the evils of implementing austerity measures in the country? Yes! Nigerians can.

CHAPTER 10

Conclusion

From January 1st 1973 to April 30th 2015, Nigerian currency (₦) has been devalued a whopping 30,500% in just a span of 42 years. Nigerians must either kill chronic corruption or be killed by it. Some centuries ago, aggressively expanding European empires identified Nigeria and other African countries as major resources in building their nations (cheap work force); Africa then became the perfect and ideal solution to build the European empire. In most cases the indigenous peoples proved unreliable and coupled with the fact that most of them were dying from diseases brought over from Europe, Europeans were also unsuited to the tropical climate of Africa and suffered some tropical diseases. Therefore, the Europeans found solace in exporting Africans to the global village. Today, millions of Africans are now paying their ways out of the continent in search of jobs and better quality of life in other developing countries.

Shortly after the first Europeans stepped their feet into the shores of Africa, they changed the dynamics of the peaceful people and murdered unity, because the level of disunity in that continent has been on an upward trajectory, maybe because of the "Divide and Conquer strategies" used by the Europeans to gain their ways into the hearts of gullible, uncivilized, innocent and unsuspecting Africans. To date, the majority of African countries remain the conquered territories of their reputed ex-colonial masters as directives and dues are still being remitted to the masters in form of repaying mysterious debts.

None of the African countries can claim to be independent; because they all *negotiated* their *independence* from the colonial masters. Therefore, African countries are simply an annex of their respective

colonial masters. A negotiated contract is just exactly what it is—
"shared common interests or jointly agreed actions and inactions."
All African countries should be seen as being partially independent
from their ex-colonial masters, because "Total Independence" comes
with bitter sacrifices and prices. Nigerians and many other African
countries never made the necessary sacrifices for independence
nor paid the required costly prices for total independence, because
freedom comes with expensive and nonnegotiable prices.

Nigerians and other Africans on the other hand were excellent
workers. They also had experience in agriculture and keeping cattle.
It was as if God fearfully and powerfully made Africans to survive in
any climate. Their resistant levels to so many diseases were amazing,
so they were found to be more than useful to work on plantations and
in mines, because they were eventually used in experimental drugs.
The solution of the carefully thought-out plans to aggressively boost
the future economic expectations of Europeans resulted in the Trans-
Atlantic Slave Trade (TAST), where fellow human beings were used
purely like animals. The Trans-Atlantic Slave Trade was one of the
ugliest ages in history, because human beings were treated worse
than animals are treated today.

Families were broken up to be sold into slavery and never to be seen
again by their loved ones, because the murdered unity gave rise to
constant boundary disputes and kidnapping people for slave trade
purposes. Nigerians and other Africans that were forcefully moved
away from the shores of Africa were distributed all over the global
village and they lost tracks of their roots; nonetheless agonies of their
forceful and unwilling separation from their loved ones were told from
one generation to the other, and such stories created big barriers for
collaboration with Africans that paid their ways into Diaspora.

Today, these groups of Nigerians and other Africans are known to
the global village as Africans At Large (AAL), and they must definitely
play a key role in reclaiming and rebuilding the continent. Any
unquestionable effort to move Nigeria and other African countries
forward must start with the coming together of Africans At Large
(AAL) and Africans In Diaspora (AID) to strategize on how best to
proceed, because committed teamwork assures success. Africans
must come together, identify common interests, strategize and make
all the necessary sacrifices to save the continent from her fri-enemies

136

(disguised predictors or oppressors), and chart a new course that will move the continent towards greatness.

Shortly after the Nigerian civil war in 1970, the corrupt politicians joined forces with the Nigerian colonial master to make sure that the country would not grow organically, and that the majority of Nigerians would be impoverished forever. Chronic corruption was allowed to grow unabated in the country because the colonial master as the watch dog of the country never saw any evil with their chosen agents of oppressions (Nigerian corrupt politicians), because any Nigerian who attempted to speak out was mysteriously killed or indirectly forced to go on self-imposed exile.

Human rights activists in the country had to scamper out of the country for fear of their lives and the externally induced cold war of suppression was unleashed on the nation's learning institutions, which resulted in the destruction of all the learning institutions in the country. Intellectualism was gradually murdered in Nigeria while fools were brought to the forefront to run the affairs of the country as desired by unseen foreign master. The unintended consequences of murdered intellectualism and learning institutions in the country gave rooms were militant groups who were disenfranchised through bad governance from the unseen forces started to grow. Some of the militant groups are now being subjugated by religious extremists fomenting trouble in our peaceful environment, since chronic corruption left some youths to easily be recruited by radical groups and men of the under-ground world economy.

The best weapon and lasting solution against the surging religious fanatics and terrorist groups in Nigeria and other Africa countries should simply be good governance. Yes! Guns and other weapons of mass destructions could be used for short-term measures, but as long as chronic corruption plays an active role, other groups will eventually emerge out of nowhere. Global village should kindly help to technically and financially support Nigeria's new government to win the war on chronic corruption and at the same time reduce the opportunities of those religious bigots that tend to capitalize in countries where there are chronic corruption to recruit and entice the unsuspecting youths. A chronically corrupt country is a futile ground for militant groups and other terrorists activities. Nigeria must collectively join forces to eradicate chronic corruption in the country or risk more terrorist militant groups, and watch as their beloved country degenerate into a safe sanctuary for more militant and terrorist groups.

Nigerian public servants and political leaders were ignorantly and indirectly allowed to misappropriate and squander the treasures the country received from high crude oil prices some years ago. Unconfirmed salary and allowances paid to Nigerian legislators show scary figures that no man on the earth can believe, because the legislators were each earning more than the president of America. As soon as Nigerian leaders sensed the depletion of the treasures, the leaders quickly rushed to IMF and World Bank to borrow more money in all-out efforts to continue their looting of the country's treasures. Nigeria is on the verge of going broke and the growth trajectory of the country has been reversed downward because of lower crude oil price and without aggressive war against chronic corruption, the country will be in a traumatic and chaotic state in the near future.

Meanwhile, in the mid-1980s, when Nigerian leaders went to borrow from International Monetary Fund (IMF) and World Bank, they were told that AUSTERITY MEASURES/ STRUCTURAL ADJUSTMENT PROGRAMS (SAP) were the only condition for the loans, totally undermining the unabated chronic corruption that caused the destruction. Incidentally, the Nigerian head of state then that came into power through military coup to save the country was the same man Muhammadu Buhari that just won the March 28th 2015 presidential election. As a true leader and one of the incorruptible Nigerians, he turned down the IMF and World Bank loan, electing to eradicate chronic corruption instead. As poor Nigerian masses were rejoicing with his decision, the same corrupt politicians connived with other military officers and overthrew his regime and accepted the IMF bank loans. As soon as the loans were accepted, the level of economic destruction in the country from 1985 took the worst turn, because the democratic institutions were totally and completely destroyed.

Meanwhile, as corruption canopied the eyes of new Nigerian leaders, the IMF's unfavorable lending agreements were immediately signed to satisfy the politicians craving appetite for looting, and as soon as the loans entered into the shores of Nigeria, the monies developed long wings and found their way back into Europeans banks under some numbered accounts. Nigerian leaders' quick acceptance of the IMF and World Bank loans actually reversed the trajectories of Nigerian growing and expanding economy into contracting economy that started killing many industries; universities, government agencies, legal and moral standards were never speared either.

The stage is now set for a rematch of what happened in Nigeria 30 years ago, when in the mid-1980s, shortly after the implementations of structural adjustment programs in Nigeria, some professionals (Medical doctors, Nurses, Engineers, etc.) and many youth left the shores of Nigeria in search of greener pastures. Those people are still finding it very difficult to return and fit into Nigerian Corporate systems, while the stage is now set for history to repeat itself in the country. Another wave of austerity measures in the country is clear and immediate and Nigerians must think outside the box to help ease the pains of the programs.

The price of crude oil had gone up from $65 to $147 between 2007 and 2012. Some Nigerian and many African countries benefited from the high crude oil price, and yet, as this book is being put together, many of these African countries are on the verge of running short of capital, and some African leaders are seriously romancing with IMF and World Bank for assistance. African countries will soon be engulfed with the implementation of another Structural Adjustment Program. Some African countries might have already accepted IMF loans but smartly disguised the implementation phase of the loans. Many economists are pointing to the recently announced subsidy withdrawals and currency devaluations of some African countries as signs of IMF and World Bank loans acceptance, the pictures will definitely be clearer in due time.

There were a series of military coups in Nigeria and African countries in the 1980s because of misappropriations of national treasuries. Nigeria and other African countries definitely cannot afford another wave of military coups in the continent. Therefore, Nigerians must join the new administration to kill chronic corruption because military coups only elevate corruption to higher dimensions. It might not be an overstatement to say that "chronic corruption was unofficially legitimized and it became acceptable means of doing business in Nigeria" and any Nigerian that refuses to partake in chronic corruption is viewed as abnormal. Now look around the country. The same indicators that piloted the country into the hopeless and terrifying situations in the 1980s are more pronounced than ever. Nigeria definitely cannot afford to be plunged back into the dark ages of the 1980s again, because that will spell doom for the country. Henceforth, Nigeria's new administration must be encouraged to vigorously pursue its agenda, especially killing off chronic corruption. Nigerians should not forget that the new president patiently waited almost 16 years for another opportunity to be a symbol of change.

Meanwhile, time is the greatest enemy to Nigerian core stakeholders because Nigerian professionals in Diaspora who would play an active role in the rebuilding process only have a few years of usefulness left in them. The Nigerian government has to fish out those Nigerian professionals in Diaspora who are not chronically corrupt and engage them to be the outside change that would not look at faces when implementing viable reforms. If the Nigerian government cannot find ways to harness the potentials of Nigerians At Large and Nigerian professionals in Diaspora, then the country will not benefit from baby-boomers, people born between 1946 to 1964, who were instrumental in building the global village. For Nigeria to gravitate towards the next engine of global growth, strong inputs are really needed from those professionals at large and professionals in Diaspora (Nigerians that paid their ways out of the country from 1970 to date).

Unless Nigerian government can speed up national building efforts, the government might never have the opportunities to harness the great potential and wealth of experiences from those professionals in Diaspora and at Large. One of the greatest advantages the country has today is the huge number of Nigerian professionals in Diaspora and those at Large (close to 10,000,000). Until the country can find meaningful ways of harnessing this asset, the country will remain 6 decades behind other countries in the global village.

Third-world and under developed countries like Nigeria can never solidly metamorphous into developing nations without harnessing or utilizing the potentials of their citizens that are in Diaspora and at Large. Secondly, the chronic corruption in the country must be reduced to manageable levels before gainful and sustainable progress will be made in the country. Chronic corruption in Nigeria has grown into a deadly and consuming monster, so powerful that Nigerian leaders alone cannot destroy the big monster with 12 heads and many unseen tails. There might be serious need to have global village be actively involved in rebuilding Nigeria because the country is the giant of the continent that brought civilization to mankind. Nigeria is in a calamitous need of all the help that the country can garner today because the deadly challenges facing the country is clear and immediate.

Yes! There is corruption all over the global village, but the chronic corruption found in Nigeria and other Africa countries is very worrisome and upsetting, because the majority of the populace is corrupt and there are no mechanisms in place for control. Chronic corruption is very devastating and destroying because it makes mockery of all the systems and sub-systems in all spheres of political, social and economic activities in Nigeria and other African countries.

If chronic corruption continues un-checked and un-abated in the continent, Nigerians and other Africans would definitely remain on the bad side of developments and history of mankind, because the man-made menace is impoverishing the continent. Having Nigeria and some African countries as the next engines of global growth might just be a wishful thinking, unless they are all willing to make the necessary painful sacrifices and institute systems that would help to eradicate chronic corruption which will tower the continent to the height of global respect.

Meanwhile, many Nigerian professionals in Diaspora have started dumping their various professions since the 2008 financial meltdown that saw the elimination of boomers jobs. The professionals are now heading to the now assumed lucrative nursing professions to make ends meet. Accountants, Lawyers, Financial Advisors, Architects, Engineers, Teachers, Salesmen and etc. are all heading to nursing program, since that is the only program that guarantee job security, unfortunately, the dumping professions would have been priceless treasures to Nigeria and other African governments if chronic corruption had not taken over the continent. Worrisome trends indeed, because the talents and experiences of these great men and women in different professions would be lost forever. Nigeria and African governments really do not have much time left to start the process of fishing out and luring back these professionals in Diaspora into the continent, because predominant number of them are from the baby-boomers generation that have started their retirement January 2011.

However, some Nigerians and African professionals in Diaspora, who are determined to go back to Africa and lend helping hands in rebuilding the continent were completely seen as strangers, and were indirectly forced to leave the continent. Nigeria the giant of the continent has gone through some traumatic changes that actually spread chronic corruption to other parts of the continent and all the countries must have to reach out to their professionals in Diaspora in genuine efforts to rebuild the continent.

Building and rebuilding of new Africa must be collective efforts of Africans at large Those in Diaspora and all African governments; the continent definitely need the help of those Africans that have been exposed to democratic and functional systems of government all over the world. Information is power, knowledge is asset, let Nigeria and other African governments kill chronic corruption, then reach out and partner with those Africans in Diaspora and jointly march towards greatness.

The reverberation of this famous quotation lingers on: "Now he has won our brothers and our clan no longer acts like one. He has put a knife on the things that held us together, and we have fallen apart." This is a quotation from Chinua Achebe's book titled, "Things Fall Apart". This book had to be referenced, because it is a summation of what is happening in modern Nigeria and many African countries. Africa was greatly divided by their colonial masters, and to date, those divisions are currently growing like undomesticated animals. Make no mistake, unless the colonial masters and other global village superpowers step in and help to unite Africans again, unity will be a completely forgotten chapter in the continent.

Look at what is happening in South Africa today because chronic corruption has taken good chunk of the leaders, and the leaders were looking for whom to blame. The political leaders finally found a way to blame the slowing down economy on the immigrants that are doing menial jobs to make ends meet, and immediately, the surging poor, unemployed and angry youths took their anger out on the poor immigrants by killing and destroying their properties. What a shameful act on South Africans, killing their fellow Africans because the evils of chronic corruption are beginning to surge in that country.

Nigeria the presumable giant of Africa is one of the most blessed countries in the world; the numerous mineral resources Mother Nature endowed on this part of the global village can demonstrate this claim, but chronic corruption has turned out to be the biggest bottleneck in all efforts to move the country forward. The fact that Nigeria does not witness catastrophic weather like hurricanes, blizzards, severe earthquakes, typhoons and tornadoes testified to Mother Nature's work in Nigeria. Nigeria must wake up from slumber, decisively deal with chronic corruption and join the rest of the countries, because Nigeria might find it very difficult to survive in this paradigm shift without speedy political and economic reforms.

In all fairness, Mother Nature was more liberal to Nigeria than any other part of the world; because the country was given everything that would make any other country great, mineral resources, vase land, a great population etc. Unfortunately for Nigeria, chronic corruption has given birth to excessive greed and envy, while some external forces in collaboration with few chronically corrupt Nigerians are doing good work in keeping the country in the worst shape anyone would not want to ask for. Christians really wonder how God would feel looking at what is happening in His powerfully and beautifully made country today, because if God asked for up to 10,000 righteous Nigerian men and women as a condition to save the country, they might not be found.

The level of politically induced divisiveness in Nigeria that was orchestrated by chronic corruption has made it impossible for any collective effort in the country. This is a mystery that Nigerians can solve because nation building requires common interests and teamwork, the country can use establishment of sporting events at all levels to address the mystery of divisiveness. Let Nigerians remember that "sports unifies, while politically induced tribal and ethnic orientation divides". Nigerians can build a global edifice that is capable of attracting world attention, but strong teamwork and eradication of chronic corruption are highly required to accomplish the complicated task.

As Nigeria was busy in the 1980s going through one of the darkest periods in her history; battling austerity measures and chronically corrupt political class, other countries were busy with researches and inventions that led to modern day technological gadgets. The difference is quite clear because most parts of the global village are now more industrialized than Nigeria. The country has now become a huge market for used obsolete electronics, used airplanes, buses, tools and other mechanical gadgets. Nigerians rely on other countries for bulk of their technological uses, because, when other countries upgrade their appliances and technologies, then the country benefits from those downgraded appliances and technologies.

Nigeria must revisit the constitution left behind by the colonial master and the 1999 constitution that was prepared in a highly chronically corrupt environment, if they are no longer in conformity with modern setting in the country, then a new inclusive constitution under the watchful eyes of Muhammuda Buhari be put in place. The new president of the country has been seen as one of the uncorrupted Nigerians capable of moving the country forward, therefore, he is in a better position to chart a new direction for marching the country into greatness.

The world is now a global village, and if the civilized world cannot assist in charting a new course for Nigeria and other African countries, then civilized economies will continue to pay indirectly, through the continuous increases in financial and economic aids, influx of millions running away from the continent and spending billions of dollars fighting terrorisms brewed in the neglected countries like Nigeria and other African countries. Like a Japanese man would say, "don't give me fish, just teach me how to fish, so I will go and catch the fish I need .The civilized world really needs to reduce the loans and all financial aids to Nigeria and other African countries, but help Africans kill chronic corruption before increasing the economic and technology transfers to the continent. Developed countries need to motivationally encourage Africans to go through those painful reforms that are required to help tower the continent into the next engine of global growth where the whole world would benefit.

Most of the financial grants, aids, and loans to Nigeria and other African countries still end up in the hands of those Nigerians and Africans that impoverished the continent. The developed countries must directly or indirectly encourage the Nigerian and other African governments to completely eradicate chronic corruption in the continent or risk continued attacks from radical groups that attract sympathy from the huge number of unemployed youths in Africa. Good governance and accountability would definitely help to bring more peaceful and safer environments in our paradigm world. The world must jointly and collectively kill terrorist's attacks by uprooting governments that engage in chronic corruption, because chronic corruption begets terror groups, militant groups and underground economies. Not eradicating chronic corruption will continue to threaten peace and stability of the global village.

The global village cannot continue to ignore a consuming region with a population of over one billion (1,100,000,000) infested with chronic corruption without severe negative economic and financial impart in their developed economies. China and India are making so much money from Nigeria and other African countries and leaving little or nothing in return. Who knows if the re-colonization or new colonization of Africa has started with these Asians economic power brokers? Americans and other less corrupt countries are finding it very difficult to do businesses in Nigeria and other African countries because even outside, American companies are constantly being monitored for signs of corrupt practices in the global village. When a chronically corrupt country empowers another chronically corrupt country, what would you think would be the fate of the powered country?

There is no doubt that Nigerians and Africans contributed immensely to the backwardness of the continent, but let us not forget that some external forces helped. Yes! The monster with 12 heads was also vital in hindering the political, economic, social and financial growth of the continent. The fact that Nigeria and African debt and population were growing faster than the continent's real GDP is still a worrisome trend that needs global village attention, because sooner or later STARVATION will engulf the continent due to chronic corruption that used some individuals to loot the treasures, falling crude oil price, rising foreign debts and the impending IMF and World Bank prescribed Austerity Measures in the continent.

Social media have completely changed the ways global villagers interact with one another. The super powers should also use the media to monitor countries that have chronic corruption and encourage them to drop the evil menace because the global village will eventually pay for it. YouTube, Face book, Google-plus, Twitter and other social networks are now influencing how human beings perceive and interpret events. On September 12th 2012, an online video on YouTube started what might go down in history as one of the worst anti-American demonstrations because an attack on American embassy at Benghazi Libya claimed the lives of four American diplomats, including the U.S. ambassador, J. Christopher Stevens. How can such barbaric acts happen in a country that America and other global forces just liberated some months ago from decades of dictatorship? Other American embassies in Arab countries were also attacked, why? It is quite unfortunate for such attacks because Nigeria and many other African countries do not want to be seen as a terrorist continent. But the religious bigots and other radical groups are using the unemployed youths to foment terrorist's attacks in the world. Funny enough most of the African countries that are safe havens for all these terror groups have been infested with chronic corruption many decades ago, while the developed countries simply ignored their oppressive leaders.

Nigeria and many African countries still remain important integral parts of the global village and the rest of the global village cannot afford to leave these countries behind; they should help to purge chronic corruption in those parts for a safe world. As the writing of this book is going on, Nigerians and Africans are still busy shopping for exit visas from all the foreign embassies on the continent to migrate away from the shores of Africa. They are being chased away by the negative effects of chronic corruption in the continent and those that cannot get exit visas out of the continent are constantly embarking on illegal voyages with dilapidated boats that end up killing them in Lampedusa, a gateway into Europe. Nigeria and all the African countries really need jobs to create African families that can afford the basic necessities of life, or there will be an implosion of massive criminal activities. Hunger and starvations will envelope the country after the looming austerity measures from IMF must have been implemented in the continent.

Can the looming austerity measures create jobs for Nigerians and other Africans? Technically No,. Actually, the best job creating program right now would be the eradication of chronic corruption that would stop the unabated looting of African treasures, because money would definitely be saved for increased capital expenditures. Nigeria will definitely see huge surge on the numbers of the unemployed because that is the essence of austerity measures (cutting down on

146

governments spending), And since the Nigerian government is the biggest employer of labor with excess and wasteful spending, the right cuts would free money for capital expenditures that would help to create jobs that could absolve the millions of unemployed youths.

Meanwhile, the civilized world should urgently do something to curb the continuous mass exodus from Nigeria and other African countries, because many of the immigrants that are already chronically corrupt will engage in corrupt and fraudulent activities once they are out of Africa. Let the civilized world collectively help Nigeria and other African countries to eradicate chronic corruption if they want to save their own countries from the menace of the deadly man-made contagious ailment.

What is happening in Nigeria today is the greatest injustice to mankind, because sooner or later the many years of indirectly encouraging chronic corruption in the country would have global effects from brewed and groomed terror groups. Nonetheless, the rest of the global village must pay directly or indirectly from many years of allowing chronic corruption to thrive unabated in the country. Military and politically selected dictators were used to destroy all the democratic institutions with chronic corruption. Now the chickens are coming back to roost. An average Nigerian child cannot boast of one square meal a day, while a child in a developed nation might eat up to 5 times a day. Do we call this justice or equitable distribution of the global village's wealth? Absolutely not, we are in a paradigm shift, no child, man, country or continent should be left behind, Nigeria must urgently be revamped to help lead Africa to the Promised Land. Oh! What a crude world of oil? Crude World of Oil is another interesting book from the author. The global income disparity of Nigerians and other Africans in relation to the global village is so huge and urgently needs international attention, unless the global village wants to see Africa as a safe haven for terrorist and religious fanatics groups.

Needless to say that Nigerian political leaders have collectively failed the electorate through embezzlements and mismanagements of scarce resources, and as such the whole world must come together to help Nigeria chart a new course for the sake of Nigerian children. The country still has not found the whereabouts of over 200 school girls abducted by a terrorist group since April 2014, may God spare the lives of those innocent girls until they are found. Thanks to

Michelle Obama (American first lady) for her unrelenting efforts in trying to find those abducted girls, she was all over CNN and the social media encouraging the world to help find the girls.

The super-powers should think of better ways to help save lives of innocent children in the future by condemning all the evil and oppressive governments in Africa to make the global village terror free, unless deaths of those innocent lives in Nigeria and other African countries are part of population control mechanism in the global village. Aids and arms have proven not to be enough. Chronic corruption and divisiveness must first be eradicated away from Nigeria, and the western world should consider transferring more technologies to Nigeria and other under-developed countries, rather than aids.

The author opined that colonial masters hurriedly left Nigeria and other African countries without restoring, rebuilding and reconstructing the peaceful relationships that once existed among Africans before the conquest of the continent. The question now in the minds of many people in the global village is "If chronic corruption and divisiveness in Nigeria and other African countries were craftily and strategically designed to make sure that nothing good could be educationally, financially, socially and economically accomplished in the continent, why?. Maybe the ex-colonial masters were fully convinced that eventually, Nigerian and other African leaders would be more than happy to invite them to come and take the countries away from them, as their chronically corrupt minds would definitely fail to move the countries forward? High profile chess game is being played behind the scene to see who will be the next major colonial master of Africa.

How can anyone explain the move by French government that sent military troops into Mali to restore another corrupt leadership regime in that country? The best practical and cost effective ways of winning the wars against Al-Qaeda and other terror groups in the world would simply be eradication of chronic corruption in countries like Nigeria and other under-developing ones. When super powers ignore the existence of chronic corruption in Nigeria and other African countries, the world invariably makes such countries fertile grounds for Al-Qaeda and other terror organizations to capitalize on the side effects of chronic corruption and exploit the gullibility and naivety of those poor masses. AL-Qaeda can never survive in a structural working system, because such system would not provide enough recruits to continue their evil attacks on innocent people. Relying on just guns and other logistics to fight terrorists would be less fruitful until the sources that brew the groups are completely cut-off in the world. All-out war on chronic corruption that would beget good governance is the unequivocal answer to everlasting peace in our global village.

Nigeria is still partially in the secondary phase of military sponsored, designed and manipulated political power transfer processes, whose philosophies, practical orientations and institutional modalities are similar to those of the colonial master. Right now, it looks like Nigeria is getting to the tail end of military political power transfer process, but the recent religious politically induced polarization in the March 28th 2015 presidential election campaign period might have created elements of debts in the end of the transfer process. The global village is watching to see how Nigerian leaders will handle the looming austerity measure that is going to shake Nigeria to the fabrics of the foundations that hold the country together.

In the event that the new president of the country fails to muster enough supports for his transformation agendas in the country, then all hell will definitely break loose, and this is why it is imperative that majority of the poor masses must support the president or risk the worst blood bath in the history of mankind. Is China going to re-colonize Nigeria and other African countries? Or are the ex-colonial masters coming back to take their former colonies? In not too distant time, the pictures will be clearer for many Nigerians and other Africans to decide, but right now, the future of Nigeria has been suspended in a clouded unpredictable outcome.

Meanwhile, some economists and financial advisers are very optimistic, that sooner or later, there will be an emergence of sunlight at the end of the darkened tunnel of Nigerian political and economic experiences. But some pragmatists, are compelled to assert that the future is foreboding, because chronic corruption and divisiveness issues that have been tormenting and destroying the country in the past have now grown even bigger, and would need collective efforts from Nigerians and global powers to stop.

The task before every Nigerian now is the aggrieved guarding of the future that is already arrested in space of secrecy, and imploding in its time capsule. Let all Nigerians hope and pray that Muhammadu Buhari will encourage all the stakeholders of Nigeria to quickly start re-negotiations of political powers with all the electorates, which would put the country in the right growth trajectory.

Finally, the global village and Nigerians must give Muhammadu Buhari and his new administration unconditional support to pull the giant of Africa away from the fast approaching clear and immediate danger, because the unintended consequences of not saving the country would be very catastrophic to our global village. The hope of saving and making Nigeria the next engine of global growth will depend on how the following bullet points are addressed in the country without any political shenanigans:

A. To quickly review the constitution, if many flaws, create another inclusive constitution that would reflect the country's diverse groups.

B. To start a process that would automatically but gradually eradicate chronic corruption in the country. The new administration must make a statement with some of the untouchables before Nigerians will take them serious.

C. Passing of urgent laws that would empower towns/villages to have politically elected chief executives that would be in charge of political, economic and financial issues.

D. Start a process that would harness the hidden treasures of Nigerian professionals in Diaspora for better and quicker transformations of the country.

E. Create regional stock exchanges and deepen Nigerian Stock Exchange to a level that would attract influx of foreign investors. No one can succeed in a capitalistic system without excess capital and some kind of financial engineering.

F. To aggressively develop all sports from amateur to professional levels and use the individual stars and superstars (ambassadors of peace) for unification programs.

G. To start investing heavily in rebuilding existing infrastructure and building new ones that would accommodate the surging population.

H. To empower the states to be in charge of the security needs of the states.

I. The government to invest a minimum of 30% of the annual budget on youths and educational learning institutions.

J. The government must cut the excessive salaries of politicians by at least 50% and the savings use for export promotions of all goods and services to reduce the massive pressure on the Naira.

K. Changing the land use acts law that would help the towns/villages to grossly monetize trillions of hidden assets in those areas.

L. To judiciously declare all Nigerians touchable and fight chronic corruption without fear or favor from the new administration.

M. Quickly decentralize Nigeria's police and empower all states to form their own police departments for accountable and efficient policing in the states.

N. Empower the Central Bank of Nigeria to be completely independent.

If the above raised points are not urgently addressed, the country might witness the emergency of powerful militant groups and organized crime families that would be challenging both the states' and federal governments leading to a possible break-down in law and order in the country. American President Barrack Obama in his 2008 presidential election campaign slogan says "Yes we can, yes we can" and he won the election even when nobody believed he could.

President Barrack Obama in his 2012 re-election bid campaign slogan was "Moving Forward", the election was held on November 6th 2012, and he won the election despite the bad state of American economy, because Americans believed in what he was doing. Nigerian leaders can introduce the same slogan? "Yes they can, yes they can build a great nation and avoid an impending ugly future" even when many people do not believe that Nigerians alone can rebuild the country because of advance level of chronic corruption?

The accountability of guarding the future of Nigeria by all Nigerians is the only flicker and glimmer of hope that the global village will see a Nigeria that is free from political and economic manipulations of those that enslaved the country, because the country remaining in the current state will no longer work.

Nigeria needs a country that will be making use of qualified professionals for important and strategic appointments, respect the rule of law, while protecting lives and properties. Nigeria must eradicate chronic corruption then bind themselves before innovations can take place in the country again. Let us all remember that civilization actually started in the great continent of Africa, and one day, the great continent will wake up from slumber to rattle the global village. Nigerians once again should be grateful to the likes of Rev. Frank Ejike Mbaka that stood up and fearlessly preached against the Goodluck Jonathan led government that made other Nigerians to start speaking out against the government. The reverend should also remember to speak out against Buhari's government if his team starts to deviate from their promises to the poor masses.

How long would the African giant continue to sleep when there is a big fire on the mountain? Yes! There is no doubt that Nigeria got all it takes to recreate the past greatness that the country once known, but without the eradication of chronic corruption and painful reforms, Nigeria might never have the opportunity to be the next engine of global growth.

Finally, Nigeria and other African countries must prepare for the impending austerity measures that will shake the countries to the fabrics of the foundations, and if the new administration fails to adequately prepare for it and show good governance to other African countries; then the one indivisible country might wind up with many sovereign states. The better prepared countries would definitely survive the carnages and move their respective countries forward.

Let us also remember that our global village is still in revolutionary mode, where a little squabble or normal brutality might lead to something big. Needless to say that no country is immune from the global revolutionary mode, because the global village is matching into the paradigm shift of "One World Order" and all countries are respectively expected to conform. Nigeria really needs a leader that can put on Martin Luther King Jr's jacket, Nelson Mandela's shoes and Barrack Obama's tenacious will power to make transparent reforms that would start moving the country towards greatness.

Let more Nigerians dream dreams that will eventually help to march the country into greatness. The global village is still in a revolutionary mood because of the increasing income disparity between the poor and the rich, therefore global leaders should be tremendously careful as even verbal words can trigger huge civil disobediences. The recent events in Xenophobia South Africa and Baltimore in America can attest the extreme anger that poverty has meted out to the less privileged in our society. Nigerians and other African political and appointed officials should be very careful in choosing their words before plunging the continent in engulfing chronic poverty, disobedience and uprisings that might be very difficult to curtail.

Nigeria really needs to stop holding down Africa, because the time has come for the giant of Africa and hope of all black people in the world to get it right. God bless Nigeria, Africa, America, and the rest of the global village as we all race into the new paradigm shift of ONE WORLD ORDER.

BIBLIOGRAPHY

Overhauling the Engine of Growth. Vivien Foster

Africans Cry for Help by Christopher Okoli

Nigeria Troubled African Giant by Christopher Okoli

Crude World of Oil by Christopher Okoli

African Dilemma by Christopher Okoli.

Africa Emerging or Tapering Continent by Christopher Okoli.

Energy Information Administration, Washington, D.C., United States

Etemad, B., J. Luciani, P. Bairoch, and J.-C. Toutain, World Energy Production 1800-1985, Librarie DROZ, Switzerland, 1991

International Energy Agency, CO2 Emissions from Fuel Combustion, Paris, France,

2010 Energy Watch Group Report.

Hadley Centre for Climate Prediction and Research, The Met Office, Bracknell,

Berkshire RG12 2SY, UK

OPEC bulletins

CIA World Fact Book

Saving Africa from the Doomsday (not yet out)

Editing by: Elegant Editing

Editor's Note:

Chronic corruption. Most of you have never heard this expression, and probably none are familiar with its prominence in Nigerian history. Chronic corruption is a very powerful battle that all Nigerians must join their forces together and overcome in order to have a more peaceful, unified state. Learn what it is, why it occurs, what can be done to eliminate it, and how to shape the future for a successful nation. Nigeria needs to stop holding down Africa, because the time has come for the giant of Africa and hope of all black people in the world to succeed. You can learn about Nigerian national banks, villages, towns, and government, the future of crude oil, and the new President. Be inspired to help make a difference in Africa by saving the continent from further corruption and detriment, by simply making Nigeria a successful nation in the new world order.

www.ingramcontent.com/pod-product-compliance
Lightning Source LLC
Chambersburg PA
CBHW021334090426
42742CB00008B/600